UNIVERSITY LIBRARY STATISTICS

Assembled for the
ARL-ACRL JOINT COMMITTEE ON UNIVERSITY
LIBRARY STANDARDS

By

ROBERT B. DOWNS
Chairman

Assisted by John W. Heussman

Published for the
ASSOCIATION OF RESEARCH LIBRARIES
and the
ASSOCIATION OF COLLEGE AND RESEARCH LIBRARIES
by the
AMERICAN LIBRARY ASSOCIATION
Chicago 1970

Originally published as a preliminary edition
in 1969 by the Association of Research Libraries

International Standard Book Number 0-8389-5251-8 (1970)

Library of Congress Catalog Card Number 70-118013

Printed in the United States of America

UNIVERSITY LIBRARY STATISTICS ASSEMBLED FOR ARL-ACRL
JOINT COMMITTEE ON UNIVERSITY LIBRARY STANDARDS

The Joint Committee on University Library Standards was appointed early in 1968 by the Association of Research Libraries and the Association of College and Research Libraries for the purpose of formulating a statement of standards on various aspects of university library operation and administration.

As a control group, fifty leading university libraries in the United States and Canada were selected. The libraries chosen are primarily those in institutions belonging to the Association of American Universities (or more specifically the Association of Graduate Schools in the AAU), supplemented by several additional ARL libraries to bring the total number to fifty. All fifty libraries cooperated in supplying data which fall into seven categories: resources, personnel, finances, space, public service, administration, and professional school libraries. These "raw" data are presented here, prior to any attempt to develop standards, because it is believed that the statistical information in itself is valuable.

The Joint Committee's original intention was to adopt a strictly pragmatic approach to its assignment. Instead of attempting to prepare a statement of ideal standards, it was agreed that a set of criteria for excellence for university libraries, based on the best current practices, should be developed. These criteria would be drawn from the facts presented herewith for the leading American university libraries. Further research, it is generally acknowledged, will be required before valid standards can be established.

Neither the Association of Research Libraries nor the Association of College and Research Libraries has taken any action on the facts assembled by the Joint Committee, nor has the Committee itself presented any recommendations for action by the sponsoring associations. At the present stage, in fact, considerable skepticism exists as to the feasibility, or even the desirability, of setting up standards for university libraries. Among the reasons are: the "institutional environment" and "mission" of individual universities vary greatly; standards applicable to comprehensive universities may be invalid for specialized institutions; and stated minima may come to be regarded as maxima, thereby impeding the growth of a given library.

Nevertheless, if one is willing to recognize that the fifty universities included in the present compilation do indeed possess the most distinguished libraries to be found in American institutions of higher education, then something of value may be learned by a study of their current status. Any university library, if it wishes, can contrast itself with the selected fifty on such bases as financial support, resources of various types, personnel, space for books, readers, and staff, and aspects of public service. Are averages unfair in measuring a particular institution? Then medians or, perhaps better still, quartile figures may be used.

For practical application in an individual library, therefore, the appended tables may assist the librarian in determining proper distribution of budget, ratio of professional to nonprofessional staff, size of book collection, space relationships, hours of service, and a variety of additional aspects of library management. He also may contrast his situation with those institutions he considers his peers or with those whose eminence he desires to emulate.

Robert B. Downs

LIST OF TABLES

SUMMARY TABLES
PAGE

I. Finances: Total Library Budget, 1968-69; Average Annual Expenditures, 1965-68 7

II. Relationship of Total Library Expenditures to Total University Expenditures for General and Educational Purposes, 1967-68 7

III. Relationship of Total Library Expenditures to Salaries and Wages: Books, Periodicals and Binding; General Expenses, 1967-68 8

IV. Student Per Capita Expenditures for Books, Periodicals, and Binding, and for Total Library Expenditures 9

V. Resources: Volumes, Volumes Added, Current Periodicals, and Microforms 10

VI. Relationship of Enrollment to Number of Volumes and to Number of Current Journals 11

VII. Personnel 11

VIII. Relationship of Total Staff and Professional Staff to Enrollment 12

IX. Relationship of Number of Seats for Readers to Total Enrollment 12

X. Relationship of the Area of Shelving for Books to the Total Volumes Held in the Library 13

XI. Relationship of Area Assigned to Staff to the Total Area of the Library, and Number of Square Feet Per Staff Member 13

XII. Space: Air-conditioned and Carpeted 14

XIII. Circulation and Public Service 14

XIV. Student Per Capita Circulation--Summary 15

INSTITUTIONAL RANK

XV. University and Library Budget and Expenditures (Institutional Rank) ... 17

XVI. Amount and Distribution of Library Expenditures (Institutional Rank) .. 20

XVII. Amount and Per Capita Library Expenditures (Institutional Rank) 23

XVIII. Library Resources: Volumes and Current Periodicals (Institutional Rank) 26

LIST OF TABLES (contd.)

		PAGE
XIX.	Library Resources: Microforms (Institutional Rank)	29
XX.	Library Staff: Number, Distribution, and Per Student (Institutional Rank)	32
XXI.	Library Staff: Number of Hours and Cost of Wages (Institutional Rank)	35
XXII.	Reader Stations and Book Shelf Area (Institutional Rank)	38
XXIII.	Staff Area; Air-conditioned and Carpeted Space (Institutional Rank)	41
XXIV.	Total and Per Capita General and Reserve Circulation; Hours Open Per Week (Institutional Rank)	44

INSTITUTIONAL DATA

XXV.	Student Enrollment and Faculty, 1967-68	48
XXVI.	Library Budget and Expenditures; University General and Educational Expenditures	51
XXVII.	Distribution of Library Expenditures, 1967-68	54
XXVIII.	Expenditures for Salaries, Wages, Books and Periodicals, Binding, 1967-68	57
XXIX.	Student Per Capita Expenditures for Books, Periodicals, and Binding and for Total Library Expenditures	60
XXX.	Library Resources--Volumes and Current Periodicals (Total Number and Per Student Capita)	63
XXXI.	Library Resources--Microforms	66
XXXII.	Personnel--Number and Distribution; Students Per Staff Capita	69
XXXIII.	Personnel--Number of Hours and Amount Spent for Hourly Wages; Staff Work Hours Per Week	72
XXXIV.	Relationship of Number of Seats for Readers to Total Enrollment	75
XXXV.	Square Feet and Linear Feet of Book Shelves; and Volumes Per Sq. Ft.	78
XXXVI.	Amount of Staff Area and Square Feet Per Staff Member	81
XXXVII.	Total and Per Capita General and Reserve Circulation	84
XXXVIII.	Public Service Data--Miscellaneous	87

LIST OF TABLES (contd.)

PAGE

LAW LIBRARIES

XXXIX.	Summary Data on Law Libraries...	91
XL.	Law Libraries: Enrollment, Faculty, Volumes and Journals (Institutional Rank)..	92
XLI.	Law Libraries: Staff (Institutional Rank).............................	94
XLII.	Law Libraries: Expenditures and Library Hours (Institutional Rank).....	96
XLIII.	Law Libraries: Enrollment, Faculty, Volumes, and Journals (Institutional Data)..	98
XLIV.	Law Libraries: Expenditures and Library Hours (Institutional Data).....	100
XLV.	Law Libraries: Staff (Institutional Data)...............................	102

MEDICAL LIBRARIES

XLVI.	Summary Data on Medical Libraries...	105
XLVII.	Medical Libraries: Enrollment, Faculty, Volumes, and Journals (Institutional Rank)..	106
XLVIII.	Medical Libraries: Staff (Institutional Rank).........................	108
XLIX.	Medical Libraries: Expenditures and Library Hours (Institutional Rank).	110
L.	Medical Libraries: Enrollment, Faculty, Volumes, and Journals (Institutional Data)..	112
LI.	Medical Libraries: Staff (Institutional Data)...........................	114
LII.	Medical Libraries: Expenditures and Library Hours (Institutional Data)..	116

MISCELLANEOUS

LIII.	Staff Eligibility, Benefits, and Status..................................	119

SUMMARY TABLES
I - XIV

TABLE I. FINANCES: TOTAL LIBRARY BUDGET, 1968-69;
AVERAGE ANNUAL EXPENDITURES, 1965-68

	No. of Libs.	Total Amount	Average	Range Low	First Quartile	Median	Third Quartile	Range High
Library Budget, 1968-69	50	147,464,633	2,949,293	970,835	1,918,357	2,529,461	3,770,971	8,500,000
Library Expenditures, 1967-68	50	141,258,935	2,825,179	1,213,743	1,727,075	2,452,836	3,547,627	8,545,393
Average Annual Library Expenditures, 1965-68	50	122,076,147	2,441,523	1,055,368	1,500,000	2,023,594	2,932,465	7,605,880

TABLE II. RELATIONSHIP OF TOTAL LIBRARY EXPENDITURES TO TOTAL UNIVERSITY
EXPENDITURES FOR GENERAL AND EDUCATIONAL PURPOSES, 1967-68

	No. of Libs.	Total Amount	Average	Range Low	First Quartile	Median	Third Quartile	Range High
Total Library Expenditures, 1967-68	50	141,258,935	2,825,179	1,213,743	1,727,075	2,452,836	3,547,627	8,545,393
University General and Educational Expenditures, 1967-68	50	4,019,632,084	80,392,641	18,140,016	50,652,000	66,492,520	118,044,290	170,757,773
Library's Percentage	50		3.5	1.6	2.8	3.6	4.8	8.6

TABLE III. RELATIONSHIP OF TOTAL LIBRARY EXPENDITURES TO
SALARIES AND WAGES: BOOKS, PERIODICALS AND BINDING;
GENERAL EXPENSES, 1967-68

	No. of Libs.	Total Amount	Average	Range Low	First Quartile	Median	Third Quartile	Range High
Total Library Expenditures, 1967-68	50	141,258,935	2,825,179	1,213,743	1,727,075	2,452,836	3,547,627	8,545,393
Salaries and Wages	50	80,832,234	1,616,645	681,019	978,685	1,300,033	1,969,416	4,987,358
Percent, Salaries and Wages	50		57.2	43.6	53.5	56.0	61.8	67.8
Books, Periodicals, and Binding	50	47,685,800	953,716	391,241	600,983	835,357	1,239,112	2,175,961
Percent, Books, Periodicals, and Binding	50		33.8	21.2	29.4	36.5	40.3	50.0
General Expense	50	10,149,072	202,981	52,295	95,425	149,103	245,363	1,055,988
Percent, General Expense	50		7.2	2.5	4.7	5.5	13.5	28.5

TABLE IV. STUDENT PER CAPITA EXPENDITURES FOR BOOKS, PERIODICALS, AND BINDING, AND FOR TOTAL LIBRARY EXPENDITURES

	No. of Libs.	Total Amount	Average	Range Low	First Quartile	Median	Third Quartile	Range High
Total Enrollment (FTE)	50	994,740	19,895	4,719	11,840	16,775	28,369	48,285
Total Library Expenditures	50	141,258,935	2,825,179	1,213,743	1,727,075	2,452,836	3,547,627	8,545,393
Per Capita, Total Library Expenditures	50		142.01	54.77	99.34	128.07	236.90	568.56
Expenditures for Books, Periodicals, Binding	50	47,685,800	953,716	391,241	600,983	835,357	1,239,112	2,175,961
Per Capita for Books, Periodicals, Binding	50		47.94	20.39	35.40	46.61	70.13	224.54

TABLE V. RESOURCES: VOLUMES, VOLUMES ADDED, CURRENT PERIODICALS, AND MICROFORMS

	No. of Libs.	Total Amount	Average	Range Low	First Quartile	Median	Third Quartile	Range High
Total Volumes, June 30, 1968	50	99,459,415	1,989,188	890,666	1,164,142	1,456,684	2,103,723	7,920,387
Gross Number of Volumes Added (3 year average)	46	4,767,687	103,645	37,268	69,001	79,867	130,523	254,311
Net Number of Volumes Added (3 year average)	49	4,566,297	93,190	11,182	64,296	75,652	119,773	251,540
Current Periodicals Received	47	692,543	14,735	5,649	9,100	11,050	17,049	50,055
Number of Microforms	47	15,957,577	339,523	7,641	160,392	349,423	455,498	924,704
Microfilm Reels	44	1,228,543	27,921	2,452	13,947	22,930	41,632	101,396
Microfiche, Microcards, Microprint	43	13,693,569	318,455	5,189	170,686	320,918	439,060	907,531

TABLE VI. RELATIONSHIP OF ENROLLMENT TO NUMBER OF VOLUMES
AND TO NUMBER OF CURRENT JOURNALS

	No. of Libs.	Total Amount	Average	Range Low	First Quartile	Median	Third Quartile	Range High
Enrollment	50	994,740	19,895	4,719	11,840	16,775	28,369	48,285
Number of Volumes	50	99,459,415	1,989,188	890,666	1,164,142	1,456,684	2,103,723	7,920,387
Volumes per Student	50		99.99	30.35	60.07	83.56	143.76	665.29
Number of Current Periodicals	47	692,543	14,734	5,649	9,100	11,050	17,049	50,055
Enrollment	47	959,314	20,411	4,719	13,299	16,903	28,651	48,285
Periodicals per Student	47		.72	.24	.46	.68	1.33	4.59

TABLE VII. PERSONNEL

	No. of Libs.	Total Amount	Average	Range Low	First Quartile	Median	Third Quartile	Range High
Professional Staff	50	4,439	88.8	33	56	73	99	227
Nonprofessional Staff	50	7,681	153.6	58	98	119	199	426
Total Staff	50	12,120	242.4	98	154	184.5	297	653
Percent Professional	50		36.6	26.7	33.1	37.6	42.0	51.3
Hourly Wages	49	6,680,305	136,332	29,164	72,068	113,000	193,351	446,628
Work Hours/Week Professionals	50	1,922	38.44	35	37.5	39.0	40.0	40
Work Hours/Week Clerical	49	1,894	38.66	35	37.5	40.0	40.0	40

TABLE VIII. RELATIONSHIP OF TOTAL STAFF AND PROFESSIONAL STAFF TO ENROLLMENT

	No. of Libs.	Total Amount	Average	Range Low	First Quartile	Median	Third Quartile	Range High
Enrollment	50	994,740	19,895	4,719	11,840	16,775	28,369	48,285
Professional Staff	50	4,439	88.8	33	56	73.0	99	227
Enrollment/Professional Staff	50		224.09	41.64	158.36	225.24	362.96	675.72
Total Staff	50	12,120	242.40	98	154	184.5	297	653
Enrollment/Total Staff	50		82.07	16.42	49.05	89.05	133.98	275.14

TABLE IX. RELATIONSHIP OF NUMBER OF SEATS FOR READERS TO TOTAL ENROLLMENT

	No. of Libs.	Total Amount	Average	Range Low	First Quartile	Median	Third Quartile	Range High
Enrollment	50	994,740	19,895	4,719	11,840	16,775	28,369	48,285
Enrollment	49	986,745	20,138	4,719	12,570	16,903	28,510	48,285
Number of Seats	49	162,074	3,308	955	2,276	3,000	4,391	7,808
Seats/Enrollment (percent)	49		16	05	12	16	26	62
Students per Seat	49		6.09	1.60	3.84	6.15	8.41	20.65

TABLE X. RELATIONSHIP OF THE AREA OF SHELVING FOR BOOKS TO THE TOTAL VOLUMES HELD IN THE LIBRARY

	No. of Libs.	Total Amount	Average	Range Low	First Quartile	Median	Third Quartile	Range High
Number of Volumes	50	99,459,415	1,989,188	890,666	1,164,142	1,456,684	2,103,723	7,920,387
Number of Volumes	37	74,389,379	2,010,524	890,666	1,178,048	1,445,229	2,357,148	7,920,387
Book Shelving Area	37	5,609,643	151,612	24,070	82,278	121,582	215,729	523,068
Volumes per Square Foot	37		13.26	7.42	9.70	13.70	16.81	49.95

TABLE XI. RELATIONSHIP OF AREA ASSIGNED TO STAFF TO THE TOTAL AREA OF THE LIBRARY, AND NUMBER OF SQUARE FEET PER STAFF MEMBER

	No. of Libs.	Total Amount	Average	Range Low	First Quartile	Median	Third Quartile	Range High
Staff Area	34	1,144,798	33,671	8,800	18,310	29,328	44,191	91,287
Number of Staff Members	34	8,343	245.38	98	162	185	293	653
Square Foot per Staff Member	34		137.22	22.72	97.21	146.68	179.76	328.76

TABLE XII. SPACE: AIR-CONDITIONED AND CARPETED

	No. of Libs.	Total Amount	Average	Range Low	First Quartile	Median	Third Quartile	Range High
Air-Conditioned Space	35	8,345,073	238,430	29,732	128,250	204,600	363,563	510,000
Carpeted Area	33	829,513	25,136	300	6,234	13,478	48,308	86,818

TABLE XIII. CIRCULATION AND PUBLIC SERVICE

	No. of Libs.	Total Amount	Average	Range Low	First Quartile	Median	Third Quartile	Range High
Recorded General Circulation	43	24,150,549	561,641	127,723	284,658	464,153	697,013	2,395,029
Recorded Reserve Circulation	40	8,462,190	211,555	15,369	59,714	166,569	342,623	647,860
Recorded General and Reserve Circulation	45	38,360,615	852,458	193,043	502,269	760,779	1,156,456	2,517,704
Number of Hours Open per Week	50	4,877.25	97.55	74	89.5	100.0	106	121.5

TABLE XIV. STUDENT PER CAPITA CIRCULATION--SUMMARY

	No. of Libs.	Total Amount	Average	Range Low	First Quartile	Median	Third Quartile	Range High
Total Enrollment	50	994,740	19,894	4,719	11,840	16,775	28,369	48,285
Total Enrollment	43	834,806	19,414	4,719	8,811	16,393	28,651	48,285
General Circulation	43	24,150,549	561,641	127,723	284,658	464,153	697,013	2,395,029
Student per Capita General Circulation	43		28.93	4.31	14.44	28.31	55.73	82.98
Total Enrollment	45	897,499	19,944	4,719	10,065	16,393	28,510	48,285
General and Reserve Circulation	45	38,360,615	852,458	193,043	502,269	760,779	1,156,456	2,517,704
Student per Capita General and Reserve Circulation	45		42.74	9.55	26.43	39.41	70.49	109.18

INSTITUTIONAL RANK
TABLES XV - XXIV

TABLE XV. UNIVERSITY AND LIBRARY BUDGET AND
EXPENDITURES (INSTITUTIONAL RANK)

University	Total Library Expenditures, 1967-68	Total Library Budget, 1968-69	Avg. Annual Library Expenditures, 1965-68	University General and Educational Expenditures, 1967-68	Library's Percentage of University G. and E. Expenditures
Brown Univ.	43	40	42	49	4
Columbia	8	9	9	7	41.5
Cornell	7	7	6	8	29.5
Duke	31	30	27	39	16
Harvard	1	1	1	4	7
Indiana[1]	18	17	20	22	22.5
Johns Hopkins	42	41	43	48	5
Louisiana State	49	49	47	43	9
M.I.T.	35	34	37	33	29.5
McGill	28	22	33	42	10.5
Michigan State	24	25	23	25	25.5
New York	23	18	19	3	50
Northwestern	26	33	28	30	18.5
Ohio State	15	11	14	9	41.5
Pennsylvania State	10	8	13	15	22.5
Princeton	20	20	24	35	10.5
Purdue	29	28	25	18	44.5
Rutgers	25	23	26	36	13
Southern Illinois	19	19	18	26	17
Stanford	6	6	7	16	14
Syracuse	38	39	36	28	37.5
Tulane	50	48	48	46	20.5
Univ. Alabama	47	47	45	32	46.5

TABLE XV. (contd.)

University	Total Library Expenditures, 1967-68	Total Library Budget, 1968-69	Avg. Annual Library Expenditures, 1965-68	University General and Educational Expenditures, 1967-68	Library's Percentage of University G. and E. Expenditures
Arizona	45	45	49	41	32
California, Berkeley	3	4	2	12	15
California, LA	4	5	3	5	25.5
Chicago	13	12	15	11	37.5
Colorado	32	31	29	47	2
Florida	36	36	34	19	48
Illinois[2]	9	10	5	10	31
Iowa	33	27	31	21	41.5
Kansas	39	35	41	45	8
Kentucky	41	44	40	23	44.5
Michigan	5	2	4	1	33
Minnesota	12	16	12	2	46.5
Missouri[3]	37	37	38	24	41.5
Nebraska	46	43	46	38	39
North Carolina	30	26	32	29	28
Oklahoma	48	50	50	50	3
Pennsylvania	21	21	21	6	49
Rochester	34	42	35	34	25.5
Southern California	40	38	39	31	35
Texas	17	32	17	40	6
Toronto	2	3	8	20	1
Virginia	44	46	44	44	12

TABLE XV. (contd.)

University	Total Library Expenditures, 1967-68	Total Library Budget, 1968-69	Avg. Annual Library Expenditures, 1965-68	University General and Educational Expenditures, 1967-68	Library's Percentage of University G. and E. Expenditures
Univ. Washington	16	14	10	14	35
Wisconsin[4]	14	13	11	13	35
Washington Univ.	27	29	30	37	18.5
Wayne State	22	24	22	27	20.5
Yale	11	15	16	17	25.5
Total Amount	141,258,935	147,464,633	122,076,147	4,019,632,084	--
No. of Libs.	50	50	50	50	50
First Quartile	1,727,075	1,918,357	1,500,000	50,652,000	2.8
Median	2,432,836	2,529,461	2,432,836	66,492,520	3.6
Third Quartile	3,547,627	3,770,971	2,932,465	118,044,290	4.8

TABLE XVI. AMOUNT AND DISTRIBUTION OF LIBRARY
EXPENDITURES (INSTITUTIONAL RANK)

University	Salaries and Wages: Amount	Salaries and Wages: Percent	Books, Per. and Binding: Amount	Books, Per. and Binding: Percent	General Expense: Amount	General Expense: Percent
Brown Univ.	40	24	41	26	34	17
Columbia	7	7.5	15	44.5	18	37.5
Cornell	6	13	7	30	12	25
Duke	32	36.5	30	23	41	41
Harvard	1	17	3	50	1	5
Indiana[1]	15	4	23	36	46	50
Johns Hopkins	38	15	49	46.5	16	2.5
Louisiana State	45	10	50	35	44	24
M.I.T.	27	6	45	41.5	30	18
McGill	25	9	34	33	40	40
Michigan State	24	36.5	20	16	15	11.5
New York	19	14	31	39	8	6
Northwestern	31	47.5	37	48	2	1
Ohio State	16	38	12	25	6	8
Pennsylvania State	17	50	2	1	11	23
Princeton	21	35	18	9	29	27
Purdue	29	30.5	28	21	17	7
Rutgers	26	43	17	4	33	35
Southern Illinois	23	41	16	8	19	21
Stanford	8	32.5	9	38	5	15.5
Syracuse	42	44	33	12.5	21	10
Tulane	49	25	48	17.5	48	32.5
Univ. Alabama	48	32.5	42	7	49	43

TABLE XVI. (contd.)

University	Salaries and Wages: Amount	Salaries and Wages: Percent	Books, Per. and Binding: Amount	Books, Per. and Binding: Percent	General Expense: Amount	General Expense: Percent
Arizona	44	29	43	22	38	22
California, Berkeley	3	2.5	6	46.5	9	29.5
California, LA	5	12	5	40	4	11.5
Chicago	14	40	13	29	7	13.5
Colorado	33	34	29	17.5	28	20
Florida	30	11	40	34	37	26
Illinois[2]	10	30.5	4	6	23	47.5
Iowa	35	39	25	5	39	37.5
Kansas	47	49	35	10.5	14	2.5
Kentucky	39	28	36	10.5	47	45
Michigan	4	2.5	8	43	13	35
Minnesota	12	27	11	27.5	31	49
Missouri[3]	43	47.5	27	2	27	13.5
Nebraska	46	26	47	24	36	19
North Carolina	28	21	26	15	43	47.5
Oklahoma	50	42	39	3	50	45
Pennsylvania	18	16	21	27.5	32	29.5
Rochester	34	19.5	44	41.5	26	15.5
Southern California	36	5	46	37	42	32.5
Texas	22	46	32	49	25	29.5
Toronto	2	18	1	31.5	3	9
Virginia	41	19.5	38	19	45	39
Univ. Washington	11	1	22	44.5	22	29.5

TABLE XVI. (contd.)

University	Salaries and Wages: Amount	Salaries and Wages: Percent	Books, Per. and Binding: Amount	Books, Per. and Binding: Percent	General Expense: Amount	General Expense: Percent
Wisconsin[4]	13	22.5	10	20	20	35
Washington Univ.	37	45	24	12.5	10	4
Wayne State	20	22.5	19	14	35	45
Yale	9	7.5	14	31.5	24	42
Total Amount	80,832,234	--	47,685,800	--	10,149,072	--
No. of Libraries	50	50	50	50	50	50
First Quartile	978,685	53.5	600,983	29.4	95,425	4.7
Median	1,300,033	56.0	835,357	36.5	149,103	5.5
Third Quartile	1,969,416	61.8	1,239,112	40.3	245,363	13.5

TABLE XVII. AMOUNT AND PER CAPITA LIBRARY
EXPENDITURES (INSTITUTIONAL RANK)

University	Total Library Expenditures: Amount	Total Library Expenditures: Per Student	Expen. for Books, Per. & Binding Amount	Expen. for Books, Per. & Binding Per Student	Total Enrollment (FTE)
Brown Univ.	43	7	41	7	49
Columbia	8	9	15	11	37
Cornell	7	10	7	9	35
Duke	31	8	30	6	47
Harvard	1	1	3	5	33
Indiana[1]	18	35	23	41	16
Johns Hopkins	42	14	49	16	46
Louisiana State	49	49	50	50	21
M.I.T.	35	12	45	14	44
McGill	28	21	34	25	34
Michigan State	24	50	20	49	2
New York	23	29	31	39	18
Northwestern	26	19	37	34	28
Ohio State	15	40	12	42	3
Pennsylvania State	10	30	2	18	5
Princeton	20	2	18	1	50
Purdue	29	45	28	43	15
Rutgers	25	43	17	37	8
Southern Illinois	19	39	16	35	11
Stanford	6	5	9	4	39
Syracuse	38	34	33	30	26
Tulane	50	24	48	19	40
Univ. Alabama	47	44	42	40	24

TABLE XVII. (contd.)

University	Total Library Expenditures: Amount	Total Library Expenditures: Per Student	Expen. for Books, Per. & Binding Amount	Expen. for Books, Per. & Binding Per Student	Total Enrollment (FTE)
Arizona	45	47	43	44	19
California, Berkeley	3	15	6	22	14
California, LA	4	16	5	21	10
Chicago	13	4	13	3	42
Colorado	32	27	29	26	23
Florida	36	31	40	38	27
Illinois[2]	9	22	4	15	12
Iowa	33	28	25	23	25
Kansas	39	32	35	29	30
Kentucky	41	26	36	24	36
Michigan	5	20	8	32	6
Minnesota	12	46	11	45	1
Missouri[3]	37	38	27	27	22
Nebraska	46	48	47	46	20
North Carolina	30	25	26	20	32
Oklahoma	48	42	39	36	29
Pennsylvania	21	18	21	17	31
Rochester	34	6	44	10	48
Southern California	40	23	46	28	38
Texas	17	37	32	47	9
Toronto	2	13	1	12	13
Virginia	44	17	38	13	41
Univ. Washington	16	41	22	48	4

TABLE XVII. (contd.)

University	Total Library Expenditures: Amount	Total Library Expenditures: Per Student	Expen. for Books, Per. & Binding Amount	Expen. for Books, Per. & Binding Per Student	Total Enrollment (FTE)
Wisconsin[4]	14	33	10	33	7
Washington Univ.	27	11	24	8	45
Wayne State	22	36	19	31	17
Yale	11	3	14	2	43
Total Amount	141,258,935	--	47,685,800	--	994,740
No. of Libraries	50	50	50	50	50
First Quartile	1,727,075	99.34	600,983	35.40	11,840
Median	2,452,836	128.07	835,357	46.61	16,775
Third Quartile	3,547,627	236.90	1,239,112	70.13	28,369

TABLE XVIII. LIBRARY RESOURCES: VOLUMES AND CURRENT
PERIODICALS (INSTITUTIONAL RANK)

University	Total No. of Volumes	Volumes Per Student	Gross No. Vols. Added (3-year Average)	Net. No. Vols. Added (3-year Average)	No. of Current Periodicals	Current Per. Per Student
Brown Univ.	36	8	44	45	43	8
Columbia	4	6	12	17	11	12
Cornell	7	10	5	3	5	6
Duke	18	5	24	23	33	9
Harvard	1	2	2	5	2	3
Indiana[1]	20	36	--	11	26	38
Johns Hopkins	22	9	23	48	27	10
Louisiana State	45	41	42	43	14	16.5
M.I.T.	44	15	20	22	46	16.5
McGill	40	27	40	41	16	14
Michigan State	28	50	--	19	20	45.5
New York	24	35	21	26	21	30.5
Northwestern	19	18	27	24	4	7
Ohio State	13	42	15	13	34	47
Pennsylvania State	38	48	16	16	35	45.5
Princeton	17	3	29	27	8	1
Purdue	49	49	37	37	18	35.5
Rutgers	25	43	19	20	36	41.5
Southern Illinois	31	44	9	8	42	44
Stanford	8	7	4	4	3	2
Syracuse	32	28	30	47	45	35.5
Tulane	46	20	46	49	--	--
Univ. Alabama	48	40	--	36	41	34

TABLE XVIII. (contd.)

	Total No. of Volumes	Volumes Per Student	Gross No. Vols. Added (3-year Average)	Net No. Vols. Added (3-year Average)	No. of Current Periodicals	Current Per. Per Student
Arizona	33	37	43	44	25	30.5
California, Berkeley	6	17	7	9	1	5
California, LA	12	24	10	10	6	18
Chicago	10	4	11	12	--	--
Colorado	37	33	--	21	17	19
Florida	35	29	38	39	32	27
Illinois[2]	3	14	3	2	10	26
Iowa	29	26	36	38	30	28
Kansas	30	25	31	29	22	20.5
Kentucky	47	32	35	34	31	22
Michigan	5	22	8	7	9	25
Minnesota	11	39	14	14	15	41.5
Missouri[3]	27	30	32	30	--	--
Nebraska	50	46	45	46	24	29
North Carolina	21	19	26	25	47	39.5
Oklahoma	39	31	39	40	40	32
Pennsylvania	14	16	22	31	23	23
Rochester	41	11	33	33	19	4
Southern California	34	21	41	42	38	20.5
Texas	15	34	17	15	39	43
Toronto	9	23	1	1	9	24
Virginia	26	12	25	28	44	15
Univ. Washington	23	47	18	18	12	37

TABLE XVIII. (contd.)

	Total No. of Volumes	Volumes Per Student	Gross No. Vols. Added (3-year Average)	Net No. Vols. Added (3-year Average)	No. of Current Periodicals	Current Per. Per Student
Wisconsin[4]	16	38	13	--	13	33
Washington Univ.	43	13	34	35	29	11
Wayne State	42	45	28	32	37	39.5
Yale	2	1	6	6	38	13
Total Amount	99,459,415	--	4,767,687	4,566,297	692,543	--
No. of Libraries	50	50	46	49	47	47
First Quartile	1,164,142	60.07	69,001	64,296	9,100	.46
Median	1,456,684	83.56	79,867	75,652	11,050	.68
Third Quartile	2,103,723	143.76	130,523	119,773	17,049	1.33

TABLE XIX. LIBRARY RESOURCES: MICROFORMS
(INSTITUTIONAL RANK)

University	No. of Microfilm Reels	No. of Microfiche, Microcards, Microprint	Total No. of Microforms
Brown Univ.	37	33	35
Columbia	3	6	6
Cornell	8	2	2
Duke	23	35	40
Harvard	11	9	10
Indiana[1]	25	25	28
Johns Hopkins	--	--	17
Louisiana State	15	31	33
M.I.T.	42	34	38
McGill	--	--	37
Michigan State	31	27	30
New York	36	7	9
Northwestern	35	30	32
Ohio State	18	21	20
Pennsylvania State	9	16	14
Princeton	13	26	27
Purdue	39	19	23
Rutgers	26	37	41
Southern Illinois	4	38	42
Stanford	17	14	16
Syracuse	27	1	1
Tulane	41	18	19
Univ. Alabama	38	27	31

TABLE XIX. (contd.)

University	No. of Microfilm Reels	No. of Microfiche, Microcards, Microprint	Total No. of Microforms
Arizona	32	39	44
California, Berkeley	1	13	8
California, LA	7	8	7
Chicago	5	36	36
Colorado	43	42	46
Florida	10	41	43
Illinois[2]	--	--	26
Iowa	14	23	24
Kansas	28	40	45
Kentucky	12	5	4
Michigan	2	17	13
Minnesota	6	24	21
Missouri[3]	--	--	--
Nebraska	44	43	47
North Carolina	20	28	29
Oklahoma	--	--	39
Pennsylvania	21	11	11
Rochester	30	--	--
Southern California	40	32	34
Texas	19	12	15
Toronto	22	20	22
Virginia	29	10	12
Univ. Washington	16	4	5

TABLE XIX. (contd.)

University	No. of Microfilm Reels	No. of Microfiche, Microcards, Microprint	Total No. of Microforms
Wisconsin[4]	34	3	3
Washington Univ.	33	22	25
Wayne State	24	15	18
Yale	--	--	--
Total Amount	1,228,543	13,693,569	15,957,577
No. of Libraries	44	43	47
First Quartile	13,947	170,686	160,392
Median	22,930	320,918	349,423
Third Quartile	41,632	439,060	455,498

TABLE XX. LIBRARY STAFF: NUMBER, DISTRIBUTION, AND
PER STUDENT (INSTITUTIONAL RANK)

University	Prof. Staff Members	Non-Prof. Staff Members	Total No. of Staff Members	Percent Pro-fessional	Prof. Staff Members Per Student	Total Staff Members Per Student
Brown Univ.	40	35.5	38.5	32	45	45
Columbia	7	3	3	46	44	47
Cornell	10	6	6	36	41	42
Duke	28.5	32.5	32	17.5	43	41
Harvard	1	1	1	33.5	48	48
Indiana[1]	14	24	22	6	19	17
Johns Hopkins	50	40	46	49	27	35
Louisiana State	42	49.5	48	4	11	6
M.I.T.	31.5	20	23	41	40	40
McGill	17	11.5	13	17.5	38	38
Michigan State	28.5	37	34	15	1	1
New York	21	10	14	17	20	30
Northwestern	23	30	27	9	30	27
Ohio State	15	22.5	20.5	8	6	5
Pennsylvania State	13	7	9	48	15	20
Princeton	24	18	19	40	49	49
Purdue	34.5	29	29.5	28	4	8
Rutgers	34.5	47	41	5	2	2
Southern Illinois	22	45.5	38.5	1	13	4
Stanford	8.5	9	8	23	47	46
Syracuse	30	25.5	24	31	22	25
Tulane	48	48	50	19.5	25	24
Univ. Alabama	45	42.5	44.5	30	11	13

TABLE XX. (contd.)

University	Prof. Staff Members	Non-Prof. Staff Members	Total No. of Staff Members	Percent Professional	Prof. Staff Members Per Student	Total Staff Members Per Student
Arizona	46	49.5	49	7	3	3
California, Berkeley	4	8	7	12	37	32
California, LA	11	11.5	11	16	29	28
Chicago	20	14.5	16	42	42	44
Colorado	41	25.5	31	44	17	19
Florida	25.5	28	25	21	26	26
Illinois[2]	5	14.5	10	3	35	29
Iowa	27	38	33	13	24	18
Kansas	37	32.5	36	26	21	22
Kentucky	38.5	42.5	42	14	23	21
Michigan	3	4	4	27	32	33
Minnesota	8.5	19	15	2	16	7
Missouri[3]	47	41	43	37	8	12
Nebraska	43	44	44.5	25	7	9
North Carolina	25.5	35.5	29.5	10.5	28	23
Oklahoma	49	45.5	47	39	5	10
Pennsylvania	18	17	18	35	36	34
Rochester	34.5	32.5	35	24	46	43
Southern California	34.5	39	37	19.5	31	31
Texas	16	21	20.5	10.5	18	14
Toronto	6	2	2	50	33	37
Virginia	44	34	40	43	34	36
Univ. Washington	12	13	12	33.5	14	15

TABLE XX. (contd.)

University	Prof. Staff Members	Non-Prof. Staff Members	Total No. of Staff Members	Percent Professional	Prof. Staff Members Per Student	Total Staff Members Per Student
Wisconsin[4]	19	16	17	38	10	16
Washington Univ.	38.5	22.5	26	45	39	39
Wayne State	31.5	27	28	29	9	11
Yale	2	5	5	22	50	50
Total Amount	4,439	7,681	12,120	--	--	--
No. of Libraries	50	50	50	50	50	50
First Quartile	56	98	154	33.1	158.36	49.05
Median	73	119	184.5	37.6	225.24	89.05
Third Quartile	99	199	297	42.0	362.96	133.98

TABLE XXI. LIBRARY STAFF: NUMBER OF HOURS AND COST OF WAGES (INSTITUTIONAL RANK)

University	No. of Hours of Wages	Amt. Spent for Hourly Wages
Brown Univ.	37	32
Columbia	7	4
Cornell	10	6
Duke	38	35
Harvard	2	2
Indiana[1]	8	7
Johns Hopkins	43	44
Louisiana State	46	20
M.I.T.	47	43
McGill	42	--
Michigan State	15	8
New York	17	--
Northwestern	21	23
Ohio State	11	14
Pennsylvania State	9	10
Princeton	49	30
Purdue	--	38
Rutgers	18	--
Southern Illinois	5	9
Stanford	22	19
Syracuse	40	41
Tulane	33	39
Univ. Alabama	25	42

TABLE XXI. (contd.)

University	No. of Hours of Wages	Amt. Spent for Hourly Wages
Arizona	23	22
California, Berkeley	4	1
California, LA	1	--
Chicago	16	--
Colorado	24	24
Florida	29	27
Illinois[2]	14	18
Iowa	31	28
Kansas	26	29
Kentucky	36	36
Michigan	6	3
Minnesota	3	5
Missouri[3]	34	34
Nebraska	27	26
North Carolina	32	31
Oklahoma	39	12
Pennsylvania	28	21
Rochester	45	33
Southern California	35	25
Texas	12	13
Toronto	48	--
Virginia	30	40
Univ. Washington	13	11

TABLE XXI. (contd.)

University	No. of Hours of Wages	Amt. Spent for Hourly Wages
Wisconsin[4]	19	15
Washington Univ.	44	37
Wayne State	20	16
Yale	41	17
Total Amount	6,680,305	80,832,234
No. of Libraries	49	44
First Quartile	72,068	97,000
Median	113,000	134,187
Third Quartile	193,351	284,753

TABLE XXII. READER STATIONS AND BOOK SHELF AREA
(INSTITUTIONAL RANK)

University	Enrollment	Number of Seats for Readers	Seating Capacity (Percent of Enrollment)	Volumes	Book Shelving Area (Sq.Ft.)	Volumes Per Sq. Ft.
Brown Univ.	48	46	10	27	13	33
Columbia	37	8	5.5	3	10	7
Cornell	35	5	5.5	6	6	19
Duke	46	19	2	14	18	14
Harvard	33	3	3	1	1	11
Indiana[1]	16	1	10	16	7	36
Johns Hopkins	45	44	17.5	--	--	--
Louisiana State	21	32	34	--	--	--
M.I.T.	43	43	14.5	33	35	5
McGill	34	27	19.5	--	--	--
Michigan State	2	15	44.5	--	--	--
New York	18	24	34	--	--	--
Northwestern	28	40	34	15	21	10
Ohio State	3	13	40	10	16	13
Pennsylvania State	5	26	46	--	--	--
Princeton	49	28	1	13	9	31
Purdue	15	20	37	36	27	26
Rutgers	8	18	37	--	--	--
Southern Illinois	11	24	42.5	22	33	8
Stanford	39	14	4	--	--	--
Syracuse	26	48	47.5	23	24	24
Tulane	40	39	14.5	34	20	34
Univ. Alabama	24	36	31.5	--	--	--

TABLE XXII. (contd.)

University	Enrollment	Number of Seats for Readers	Seating Capacity (Percent of Enrollment)	Volumes	Book Shelving Area (Sq.Ft.)	Volumes Per Sq. Ft.
Arizona	19	45	47.5	24	34	6
California, Berkeley	14	9	26	5	4	17.5
California, LA	10	12	29	9	8	25
Chicago	42	33	12	--	--	--
Colorado	23	42	42.5	28	37	1
Florida	27	30	26	26	25	20
Illinois[2]	12	16	31.5	2	5	9
Iowa	25	21	19.5	20	23	21
Kansas	30	35	29	21	17	28
Kentucky	36	22	13	35	19	35
Michigan	6	4	21	4	3	15
Minnesota	1	2	29	8	2	37
Missouri[3]	22	24	23.5	--	--	--
Nebraska	20	34	37	37	26	27
North Carolina	32	7	7.5	17	29	4
Oklahoma	29	29	22	29	30	16
Pennsylvania	31	10	10	--	--	--
Rochester	47	49	23.5	30	36	3
Southern California	38	31	16	25	15	32
Texas	9	6	26	11	11	28
Toronto	13	47	49	7	32	2
Virginia	41	41	17.5	19	14	30
Univ. Washington	4	11	40	18	22	12

TABLE XXII. (contd.)

University	Enrollment	Number of Seats for Readers	Seating Capacity (Percent of Enrollment)	Volumes	Book Shelving Area (Sq.Ft.)	Volumes Per Sq. Ft.
Wisconsin[4]	7	17	40	12	12	22
Washington Univ.	44	38	7.5	32	28	23
Wayne State	17	37	44.5	31	31	17.5
Yale	--	--	--	--	--	--
Total Amount	986,745	162,074	--	74,389,379	5,609,643	--
No. of Libraries	49	49	49	37	37	37
First Quartile	12,570	2,276	12	1,178,048	82,278	9.70
Median	16,903	3,000	16	1,445,229	121,582	13.70
Third Quartile	28,510	4,391	26	2,357,148	215,729	16.81

TABLE XXIII. STAFF AREA; AIR-CONDITIONED AND CARPETED SPACE
(INSTITUTIONAL RANK)

University	Amt. of Staff Area (Sq. Ft.)	Total No. of Staff Members	Sq. Ft. Per Staff Member
Brown Univ.	19	28.5	8
Columbia	31	3	34
Cornell	6	5	20
Duke	16	23	10
Harvard	1	1	18
Indiana[1]	5	14	5
Johns Hopkins	--	--	--
Louisiana State	--	--	--
M.I.T.	26	15	25
McGill	--	--	--
Michigan State	--	--	--
New York	--	--	--
Northwestern	--	--	--
Ohio State	10	12.5	14
Pennsylvania State	13	6	27
Princeton	11	11	17
Purdue	15	20.5	11
Rutgers	--	--	--
Southern Illinois	25	28.5	19
Stanford	--	--	--
Syracuse	23	16	33
Tulane	21	34	3
Univ. Alabama	--	--	--

TABLE XXIII. (contd.)

University	Amt. of Staff Area (Sq. Ft.)	Total No. of Staff Members	Sq. Ft. Per Staff Member
Arizona	--	--	--
California, Berkeley	--	--	--
California, LA	--	--	--
Chicago	--	--	--
Colorado	30	22	30
Florida	32	17	31
Illinois[2]	17	7	28
Iowa	12	24	6
Kansas	18	26	9
Kentucky	14	31	4
Michigan	2	4	15
Minnesota	3	9	2
Missouri[3]	29	32	23
Nebraska	24	33	13
North Carolina	27	20.5	22
Oklahoma	--	--	--
Pennsylvania	--	--	--
Rochester	34	25	32
Southern California	20	27	12
Texas	8	12.5	7
Toronto	4	2	24
Virginia	7	30	1
Univ. Washington	22	8	29

TABLE XXIII. (contd.)

University	Amt. of Staff Area (Sq. Ft.)	Total No. of Staff Members	Sq. Ft. Per Staff Member
Wisconsin[4]	9	10	16
Washington Univ.	23	18	21
Wayne State	28	19	26
Yale	--	--	--
Total Amount	1,144,798	8,343	--
No. of Libraries	34	34	34
First Quartile	18,310	162	97.21
Median	29,328	185	146.68
Third Quartile	44,191	293	179.76

TABLE XXIV. TOTAL AND PER CAPITA GENERAL AND RESERVE CIRCULATION;
HOURS OPEN PER WEEK (INSTITUTIONAL RANK)

-44-

University	Total Enroll-ment	General Circulation	Per Student General Circulation	Reserve Circula-tion	Total Enroll-ment	General and Reserve Circulation	Per Student General and Reserve Circulation	Hours Open Per Week
Brown University	42	33	9	25	44	37	9	17
Columbia	30	8	5	2	32	6	3	46.5
Cornell	28	10	12	4	30	11	6	8
Duke	40	31	13	21	42	36	11	25.5
Harvard	--	--	--	--	28	14	14	45
Indiana[1]	--	--	--	--	15	9	19	5
Johns Hopkins	39	39	29	34	41	42	34	3
Louisiana State	18	38	41	40	20	43	44	15
M.I.T.	37	36	21	33	39	39	28	20
McGill	--	--	--	--	29	20	17	46.5
Michigan State	2	21	39	9	2	18	41	17
New York	15	28	32	5	17	19	26	39.5
Northwestern	23	40	40	28	24	40	42	43
Ohio State	--	--	--	--	3	8	30	11
Pennsylvania State	4	13	30	29	5	23	40	9.5
Princeton	43	26	1	23	45	33	1	12.5
Purdue	13	27	36	14	14	25	37	4

TABLE XXIV. (contd.)

University	Total Enrollment	General Circulation	Per Student General Circulation	Reserve Circulation	Total Enrollment	General and Reserve Circulation	Per Student General and Reserve Circulation	Hours Open Per Week
Rutgers	7	43	43	--	--	--	--	9.5
Southern Illinois	10	9	24	18	10	15	29	6.5
Stanford	32	12	7	10	34	13	5	32
Syracuse	--	--	--	--	--	--	--	36
Tulane	33	20	11	39	35	32	15	37
Univ. Alabama	20	15	16	--	--	--	--	24
Arizona	16	29	31	12	18	24	32	12.5
California, Berkeley	--	--	--	--	13	2	8	13.1
California, LA	9	2	6	17	9	3	12	22
Chicago	35	18	8	7	37	17	2	41
Colorado	19	14	5	22	21	22	21	2
Florida	22	6	10	38	23	16	16	20
Illinois[2]	11	7	19	1	11	4	18	43
Iowa	21	35	34	20	22	38	35	1
Kansas	25	25	26	24	26	31	31	48.5
Kentucky	29	41	38	37	31	44	43	6.5
Michigan	5	3	22.5	13	6	10	27	23
Minnesota	1	11	33	8	1	12	38	33.5
Missouri[3]	--	--	--	--	--	--	--	20

-45-

TABLE XXIV. (contd.)

University	Total Enrollment	General Circulation	Per Student General Circulation	Reserve Circulation	Total Enrollment	General and Reserve Circulation	Per Student General and Reserve Circulation	Hours Open Per Week
Nebraska	17	42	42	36	19	45	45	48.5
North Carolina	27	19	20	30	27	28	25	35
Oklahoma	24	17	17	32	25	26	24	17
Pennsylvania	26	23	22.5	--	--	--	--	28.5
Rochester	41	24	3	27	43	29	4	39.5
Southern California	31	32	25	19	33	35	22	50
Texas	8	1	1	26	8	1	7	33.5
Toronto	12	5	18	6	12	7	20	30
Virginia	34	37	28	31	36	41	33	27
Univ. Washington	3	4	27	3	4	5	23	38
Wisconsin[4]	6	22	35	11	7	21	36	14
Washington Univ.	38	14	14	15	40	34	13	25.5
Wayne State	14	30	37	16	16	30	39	43
Yale	36	16	4	35	38	27	10	28.5
Total Amount	834,806	24,150,549	--	8,462,190	897,499	38,360,615	--	4,877.25
No. of Libraries	43	43	43	40	45	45	45	50
First Quartile	8,811	284,658	14.44	59,714	10,065	502,269	26.43	89.5
Median	16,393	464,153	28.31	166,569	16,393	760,779	39.41	100.0
Third Quartile	28,651	697,013	55.73	342,623	28,510	1,156,456	70.49	106.0

-46-

INSTITUTIONAL DATA
TABLES XXV - XXXVIII

TABLE XXV. STUDENT ENROLLMENT AND FACULTY, 1967-68

University	Undergraduate Enrollment	Master's Candidates	Prof. Degree Candidates	Doctoral Candidates	Other Students	Total Enrollment	Total Faculty (Instr. or above) (FTE)
Brown Univ.	3,603	1,091	--	215	--	4,909	574
Columbia	5,115	4,774	1,555	1,198	657	13,299	2,505[32]
Cornell	9,618	2,880	633	1,339	--	14,470	1,560[33]
Duke	4,535	165[12]	978	169[12]	671	6,518[12]	1,128
Harvard	4,834	1,316	4,389	2,909	1,582	15,030	3,188
Indiana[1]	19,247	4,897	632	2,322	--	27,098	1,423
Johns Hopkins	4,183[5]	365[13]	696	1,559	--	7,303[5,13]	1,601
Louisiana State	15,740	1,859	677	642	273	19,191	1,025
M.I.T.	3,857	1,212	223	1,897	499[29]	7,688[29]	1,206
McGill	6,803	1,675	3,599	1,020	1,472	14,569	1,159
Michigan State	35,325	6,986	335	3,303	--	45,949	2,097
New York	22,292[6]	--	--	--	--	22,292	4,095[34]
Northwestern	9,144[7]	3,842[7]	1,441[7]	--	1,604	16,031	919
Ohio State	33,073	2,494	2,916	2,149	0	40,632	2,030
Pennsylvania State	27,925	4,659	87	--	2,978	35,649	2,464
Princeton	3,200	260	0	1,146	113	4,719	741
Purdue	18,099	8,171[14]	210	1,324[14]	--	27,804[14]	2,112
Rutgers	25,736[8]	2,420[15]	--	1,503[26]	--	29,659[8,15,26]	1,678
Southern Illinois	24,256	2,286	--	619	1,513	28,674	1,300
Stanford	5,918	5,400[16]	--	--	--	11,318	1,251
Syracuse	11,499	3,950	320	383	494	16,646	1,200
Tulane	3,874	404	1,278	745	2,510	8,811	976
Univ. Alabama	13,735	3,281[16]	--	--	--	17,016	600

-49-
TABLE XXV. (contd.)

University	Undergraduate Enrollment	Master's Candidates	Prof. Degree Candidates	Doctoral Candidates	Other Students	Total Enrollment	Total Faculty (Instr.) or above) (FTE)
Arizona	16,784[9]	2,932[17]	543	--	--	20,259[9]	1,103[35]
California, Berkeley	17,616[10]	3,320[18]	2,690	4,012[27]	181	27,819[10,18,27]	1,953
California, LA	18,960	3,677	2,559	3,874	0	29,070	1,777
Chicago	2,538	1,848	1,712	2,125	252	8,475	1,080
Colorado	13,603	2,924[19]	504	--	76	17,107[19]	979
Florida	14,898	924	370	172	29	16,393	1,801
Illinois[2]	21,643	2,795	890	3,221	102	28,651	2,650
Iowa	11,384	[20]	1,152	4,060	307	16,903[20]	1,692
Kansas	12,997	1,891	--	945	--	15,833	960
Kentucky	9,966	839	2,241	501	--	13,597	1,033
Michigan	21,593	5,174	4,219	4,159	--	35,145	1,961
Minnesota	38,651	3,664	1,892	3,541	537	48,285	4,832
Missouri[3]	18,140[11]	--	--	--	--	18,140[11]	1,200
Nebraska	16,400	704	202	155	2,754	20,215	553
North Carolina	10,845	2,249	998	1,499	--	15,591	1,127
Oklahoma	12,452	3,528[21]	--	--	--	15,980[21]	492
Pennsylvania	7,025	5,547[22]	2,069	--	1,139	15,780[22]	2,027[36]
Rochester	3,710	540	300	541	515	5,606	1,274
Southern California	6,554	2,871	1,104	618	693	11,840	1,341
Texas	24,945	1,815	1,503[25]	1,263	--	29,526[25]	1,200
Toronto	17,897	2,291	6,468	1,513	200	28,369	3,128[37]
Virginia	4,821	2,473[23]	1,276	--	--[30]	8,570[23]	754
Univ. Washington	27,485	6,025	1,007	443	3,502	38,462	1,971

TABLE XXV. (contd.)

University	Under-graduate Enrollment	Master's Candidates	Prof. Degree Candidates	Doctoral Candidates	Other Students	Total Enrollment	Total Faculty (Instr. or above) (FTE)
Wisconsin[4]	22,863	4,814	1,074	4,249	497	33,497	2,163
Washington Univ.	3,816	1,611	764	73	1,239	7,503	1,064
Wayne State	17,803	4,136[24]	1,707	697[28]	561[31]	24,904[24,28,31]	1,257
Yale	4,010	920	474	2,245	346	7,995	1,300
Total	711,010	134,399	57,687	64,348	27,296	994,740	79,504
No. of Universities	50	47	40	39	29	50	50
Average	14,220	2,860	1,442	1,650	941	19,895	1,590

TABLE XXVI. LIBRARY BUDGET AND EXPENDITURES; UNIVERSITY GENERAL AND EDUCATIONAL EXPENDITURES

University	Total Library Budget, 1968-69	Average Annual Library Expenditures, 1965-68	University Gen. and Ed. Expenditures, 1965-66	University Gen. and Ed. Expenditures, 1966-67	University Gen. and Ed. Expenditures, 1967-68	Percent of Univ. G.&E. Expenditure for Library's 1967-68 Total Expen.
Brown Univ.	1,785,955	1,346,541	18,499,948	20,703,092	23,565,657	6.7
Columbia	4,281,020	3,760,995	117,649,140	134,375,780	134,375,780[51]	2.6[45]
Cornell	4,715,686	4,083,695	106,205,296	119,047,691	133,527,266	3.4
Duke	2,232,531	1,966,643	36,383,665	43,574,761	48,214,953	4.3
Harvard	8,500,000	7,605,880[41]	121,110,731	140,944,971	154,906,071	5.5
Indiana[1,44]	3,071,196	2,484,000	54,920,000	63,849,000	74,302,000	3.7
Johns Hopkins[38]	1,701,039	1,306,923	20,455,456	23,179,934	25,335,152	6.5
Louisiana State	1,205,510	1,148,720	37,806,300	42,372,782	42,372,782[51]	5.1[45]
M.I.T.	2,131,804	1,590,574	41,660,000	48,758,000	54,652,000	3.4
McGill	2,699,200	1,784,196	31,639,116	37,722,686	42,390,722	5.0
Michigan State	2,543,922	2,199,186	53,951,392	62,210,250	69,396,283	3.6
New York	2,867,457	2,537,921	121,629,913	143,236,435	158,964,516	1.6
Northwestern	2,181,550	1,885,185	48,250,541	53,063,870	59,119,373	4.1
Ohio State	4,037,525	2,916,180	99,446,314	116,074,852	132,726,627	2.6
Pennsylvania State	4,502,000	2,932,465	79,014,716	94,697,574	108,524,197	3.7
Princeton	2,804,517	2,181,519	46,252,508	48,930,409	52,188,170	5.0

-52-

TABLE XXVI. (contd.)

University	Total Library Budget, 1968-69	Average Annual Library Expenditures 1965-68	University Gen. and Ed. Expenditures, 1965-66	University Gen. and Ed. Expenditures, 1966-67	University Gen. and Ed. Expenditures, 1967-68	Percent of Univ. G.&E. Expenditure for Library's 1967-68 Total Expen.
Purdue	2,262,435	2,048,214	69,137,514	78,962,683	92,682,408	2.3
Rutgers	2,624,120	1,998,974	39,736,593	44,757,092	51,658,015	4.8
Southern Illinois	2,820,736	2,566,149	50,375,602	54,548,000	63,588,757	4.2
Stanford	5,000,000	4,017,648	82,000,000	94,000,000	101,000,000	4.7
Syracuse	1,910,000	1,612,221	56,487,307	59,053,000	62,154,000	2.8
Tulane	1,284,060	1,107,594	26,226,000	28,538,000	30,850,000	4.0
Univ. Alabama	1,400,320	1,161,641	43,271,272	56,374,965	56,374,965[51]	2.2[45]
Arizona	1,630,485	1,093,495	35,401,000	39,055,000	45,925,000	3.1
California, Berkeley	5,593,999	5,045,072	98,869,267	110,702,163	119,534,026	4.6
California, LA	5,199,608	4,636,868	111,437,024	127,136,387	149,800,000	3.6
Chicago	4,014,624	2,911,717	102,021,695[42]	115,546,550[42]	125,154,159	2.8
Colorado	2,215,200	1,874,036	20,077,421	23,462,039	27,613,571	7.4
Florida	2,066,632	1,700,444	57,219,165	69,896,062	89,653,598	2.0
Illinois[2]	4,150,722	4,561,553	146,239,585	162,117,702	128,539,523	3.2
Iowa	2,345,788	1,816,717	60,018,296	69,059,853	77,858,666	2.6
Kansas	2,066,805	1,419,399	23,822,972	27,184,212	31,037,633	5.4
Kentucky	1,633,890	1,449,764	54,721,954	78,425,319	70,356,158	2.3

TABLE XXVI. (contd.)

University	Total Library Budget, 1968-69	Average Annual Library Expenditures, 1965-68	University Gen. and Ed. Expenditures, 1965-66	University Gen. and Ed. Expenditures, 1966-67	University Gen. and Ed. Expenditures, 1967-68	Percent of Univ. G.&E. Expenditure for Library's 1967-68 Total Expen.
Michigan	5,729,649	4,624,614	136,549,078	160,447,768	170,757,773	3.0
Minnesota	3,476,066	3,033,801	119,719,546	164,094,236	162,900,237	2.2
Missouri[3]	2,033,000	1,500,000	--	--	69,699,000	2.6
Nebraska[39]	1,684,779	1,157,812	35,599,328	41,222,273	50,652,000[47]	2.7
North Carolina	2,515,000	1,804,678	47,000,000	54,000,000	60,000,000	3.5
Oklahoma	970,835	1,055,368	14,105,382[43]	15,848,725	18,140,016[48]	7.3
Pennsylvania	2,800,000	2,278,900	102,485,566	119,673,540	135,554,757	1.9
Rochester	1,689,932	1,647,751	45,341,129	53,071,970	53,071,970[51]	3.6
Southern California	1,918,357	1,499,413	41,535,201	48,503,381	58,241,463	2.9
Texas	2,198,961	2,604,044	34,564,146	40,420,725	47,675,700	6.3
Toronto	5,718,375[40]	3,874,864[40]	48,022,000	53,466,000	78,221,000	8.6
Virginia	1,425,976	1,287,070	21,148,900	27,403,200	31,604,605	4.9
Univ. Washington	3,717,898	3,105,529	85,470,164	99,394,466	111,816,414	2.9
Wisconsin[4]	3,770,971	3,055,437	119,679,000	123,074,005	118,044,290	2.9
Washington Univ.	2,247,301	1,841,218	40,134,911	46,560,547	51,584,328	4.1
Wayne State	2,557,197	2,203,529	44,072,937	51,808,139	63,453,503	4.0
Yale	3,500,000	2,750,000	78,986,389	89,939,445	99,900,000	3.6
Total	147,464,633	122,076,147	3,126,351,385	3,620,489,534	4,019,632,084	--
No. of Libraries	50	50	49	49	50	50
Average	2,949,293	2,441,523	63,803,089	73,887,541	80,392,641	3.5

-53-

TABLE XXVII. DISTRIBUTION OF LIBRARY EXPENDITURES, 1967-68

University	Salaries and Wages		Books, Per., Binding		General Expense		Total Library Expenditures
	Amount	Percent of Total Expenditures	Amount	Percent of Total Expenditures	Amount	Percent of Total Expenditures	
Brown Univ.	887,659	56.4	571,603	36.3	114,416	7.3	1,573,678
Columbia	2,667,624	63.4	1,144,804	27.2	196,716	4.7	4,205,827
Cornell	2,777,534	61.8	1,467,023	32.7	249,661	5.6	4,494,219
Duke	1,110,495	53.8	779,742	37.8	89,085	4.3	2,064,748
Harvard	4,987,358	58.4	1,809,880	21.2	1,055,988	12.4	8,545,393[46]
Indiana[1]	1,845,625	66.4	864,753	31.1	70,000	2.5	2,780,378
Johns Hopkins	978,685	59.7	433,000	26.4	229,017	14.0	1,640,702
Louisiana State	778,597	62.7	391,241	31.5	72,122	5.8	1,241,960
M.I.T.	1,210,368[56]	64.3	536,090	28.5	136,490	7.2	1,882,945
McGill	1,340,607	63.3	682,860	32.3	92,849	4.4	2,116,316
Michigan State	1,354,756	53.8	981,194	39.0	231,434	9.2	2,516,707
New York	1,530,200[52]	60.0	739,597	29.0	280,537	11.0	2,550,334
Northwestern	1,117,849	45.6	634,508	25.9	699,383	28.5	2,451,740
Ohio State	1,841,472	53.5	1,262,545	36.7	335,465	9.8	3,439,482
Pennsylvania State	1,726,667	43.6	1,980,443	50.0	257,350	6.5	3,964,460
Princeton	1,407,986	54.0	1,059,620	40.7	139,041	5.3	2,606,647
Purdue	1,145,220	54.5	806,947	38.4	208,798	9.9	2,100,965

TABLE XXVII. (contd.)

University	Salaries and Wages Amount	Percent of Total Expenditures	Books, Per., Binding Amount	Percent of Total Expenditures	General Expense Amount	Percent of Total Expenditures	Total Library Expenditures
Rutgers	1,259,458[52]	51.3	1,076,261	43.9	118,213	4.8	2,453,932
Southern Illinois	1,378,272	51.8	1,100,574	41.4	179,364	6.7	2,658,210
Stanford	2,563,586	54.3	1,385,919	29.4	361,605	7.7	4,717,901
Syracuse	867,881	50.3	696,357	40.3	162,837	9.4	1,727,075
Tulane	687,597	56.2	475,441	38.9	60,129	4.9	1,223,167
Univ. Alabama	732,486[54]	54.3	561,045	41.6	55,338	4.1	1,348,869
Arizona	793,892	55.1	552,960	38.3	95,425	6.6	1,441,952
California, Berkeley	3,757,592	67.7	1,467,899	26.4	274,937	5.0	5,550,428
California, LA	3,313,446[52]	62.3	1,534,932	28.9	491,222	9.2	5,319,670
Chicago	1,862,755[56]	52.5	1,239,112	35.0	283,684[61]	8.0	3,547,627
Colorado	1,105,834	54.2	792,922	38.9	141,933	7.0	2,040,689
Florida	1,125,074	62.4	580,349	32.2	96,807	5.4	1,802,231
Illinois[2]	2,223,862	54.5	1,699,351	41.7	154,766	3.8	4,077,979
Iowa	1,070,091	53.2	846,648	42.1	94,643	4.7	2,011,382
Kansas	757,551	45.3	678,677	40.6	234,748	14.0	1,670,976
Kentucky	917,887	55.5	670,878	40.6	64,195	3.9	1,652,960
Michigan	3,494,917	67.7	1,421,363	27.5	245,363[60]	4.8	5,161,643
Minnesota	2,014,368	55.7	1,304,447	36.0	132,092	3.6	3,619,178

TABLE XXVII. (contd.)

University	Salaries and Wages Amount	Percent of Total Expenditures	Books, Per., Binding Amount	Percent of Total Expenditures	General Expense Amount	Percent of Total Expenditures	Total Library Expenditures
Missouri[3]	822,000	45.6	810,000	45.0	145,000	8.0	1,802,000
Nebraska	760,275	55.8	509,987[58]	37.1	96,903	7.1	1,362,166[47]
North Carolina	1,186,748	56.8	824,065	39.4	80,227	3.8	2,091,040
Oklahoma	681,019	51.4	592,125	44.7	52,295	3.9	1,325,439
Pennsylvania	1,536,946	59.1	935,441	36.0	129,403	5.0	2,601,790
Rochester	1,095,494	57.0	546,978	28.5	148,487	7.7	1,921,125
Southern California	1,068,795	64.4	510,163	30.7	81,159	4.9	1,660,117
Texas	1,399,778	46.5	698,785[59]	23.2	149,718	5.0	3,013,128
Toronto	3,877,013	57.7	2,175,961[57]	32.4	644,468	9.6	6,720,501[49]
Virginia	884,887	57.0	600,983	38.7	70,203	4.5	1,551,167
Univ. Washington	2,165,647	67.8	870,359	27.2	158,295	5.0	3,194,301
Wisconsin[4]	1,969,416	56.6	1,341,449	38.6	168,588	4.8	3,479,453
Washington Univ.	1,010,611	47.2	862,377	40.3	267,660	12.5	2,140,648
Wayne State	1,443,354	56.6	1,008,142	39.5	99,013	3.9	2,550,985
Yale	2,295,000	63.4	1,173,000	32.4	152,000	4.2	3,620,000
Total	80,832,234	--	47,685,800	--	10,149,072	--	141,258,935
No. of Libraries	50	50	50	50	50	50	50
Average	1,616,645	57.2	953,716	33.8	202,981	7.2	2,825,179

-56-

TABLE XXVIII. EXPENDITURES FOR SALARIES, WAGES, BOOKS
AND PERIODICALS, BINDING, 1967-68

University	Salaries	Wages	Books and Periodicals	Binding
Brown Univ.	779,502	108,157	527,355	44,248
Columbia	2,261,859	405,765	990,224	154,580
Cornell	2,426,973	350,561	1,319,927	147,096
Duke	1,018,101	92,394	701,796	77,946
Harvard	4,428,092	559,266	1,518,771	291,109
Indiana[1]	1,510,625	335,000	715,872	48,881
Johns Hopkins	932,985	45,700	384,111	48,889
Louisiana State	611,310	167,287	326,241	65,000
M.I.T.	1,147,418	62,950	495,370	40,720
McGill	1,340,607	[53]	621,260	61,600
Michigan State	1,035,317	319,439[55]	903,227	77,967
New York	[52]	[52]	637,584	102,013
Northwestern	986,967	130,882	525,140	109,368
Ohio State	1,598,591	242,881	1,211,595	50,950
Pennsylvania State	1,428,080	298,587	1,839,601	140,842
Princeton	1,291,322	116,664	1,008,035	51,585
Purdue	1,066,077	79,143	727,163	79,784
Rutgers	[52]	[52]	989,590	86,671
Southern Illinois	1,067,420	310,852	1,035,468	65,106
Stanford	2,364,926	198,660	1,217,840	168,079
Syracuse	794,896	72,985	637,513	58,844
Tulane	609,052	78,545	437,023	38,418
Univ. Alabama	663,218	69,268[54]	510,815	50,230

TABLE XXVIII. (contd.)

University	Salaries	Wages	Books and Periodicals	Binding
Arizona	656,400	137,492	512,197	40,763
California, Berkeley	3,074,309	683,283	1,231,588	236,311
California, LA	52	52	1,321,360	213,572
Chicago	53	53	1,009,619	229,493
Colorado	975,952	129,882	722,941	69,981
Florida	1,003,681	121,393	523,871	56,478
Illinois[2]	2,020,593	203,269	1,573,111	126,240
Iowa	951,180	118,911	771,943	74,705
Kansas	639,564	117,987	643,063	35,614
Kentucky	834,858	83,029	620,606	50,272
Michigan	2,970,882	524,035	1,240,368	180,995
Minnesota	1,649,797	364,571	1,186,982	117,465
Missouri[3]	725,000	97,000	740,000	70,000
Nebraska	636,819	123,456	469,032	35,955[58]
North Carolina	1,073,180	113,568	731,899	92,166
Oklahoma	404,647	276,372	557,830	34,295
Pennsylvania	1,378,966	157,980	786,518	148,923
Rochester	990,795	104,699	471,484	75,494
Southern California	941,451	127,344	463,073	47,090
Texas	1,155,137	244,641	643,160	55,625[59]
Toronto	3,877,013	53	53	53
Virginia	806,072	78,815	543,961	57,022
Univ. Washington	1,880,894	284,753	716,641	153,718

TABLE XXVIII. (contd.)

University	Salaries	Wages	Books and Periodicals	Binding
Wisconsin[4]	1,743,749	225,667	1,244,714	96,735
Washington Univ.	930,023	80,588	794,964	67,413
Wayne State	1,221,177	222,177	950,004	58,138
Yale	2,075,000	220,000	1,027,000	146,000
Amount	63,980,477	8,885,898	40,779,450	4,730,389
No. of Libraries	46	44	49	49
Average	1,390,880	201,952	832,234	96,538

TABLE XXIX. STUDENT PER CAPITA EXPENDITURES FOR BOOKS, PERIODICALS, AND BINDING AND FOR TOTAL LIBRARY EXPENDITURES

University	Total Enrollment (FTE)	Total Library Expenditures	Per Capita Total Library Expenditures	Expenditures for Books, Per. Binding	Per Capita Expen. for Books, Per. Binding
Brown Univ.	4,909	1,573,678	320.57	571,603	116.44
Columbia	13,299	4,205,827	316.25	1,144,804	86.08
Cornell	14,470	4,494,219	310.59	1,467,023	101.38
Duke	6,518[12]	2,064,748	316.78	779,742	119.63
Harvard	15,030	8,545,393[46]	568.56	1,809,880	120.42
Indiana[1]	27,098	2,780,378	102.60	864,753	31.91
Johns Hopkins	7,303[5,13]	1,640,702	224.66	433,000	59.29
Louisiana State	19,191	1,241,960	64.72	391,241	20.39
M.I.T.	7,688[29]	1,882,945	244.92	536,090	69.73
McGill	14,569	2,116,316	145.26	682,860	46.87
Michigan State	45,949	2,516,707	54.77	981,194	21.35
New York	22,292	2,550,334	114.41	739,597	33.18
Northwestern	16,031[7]	2,451,740	152.94	634,508	39.58
Ohio State	40,632	3,439,482	84.65	1,262,545	31.07
Pennsylvania State	35,649	3,964,460	111.21	1,980,443	55.56
Princeton	4,719	2,606,647	552.37	1,059,620	224.54
Purdue	27,804[14]	2,100,965	75.56	806,947	29.02
Rutgers	29,659[8,15,26]	2,453,932	82.74	1,076,261	36.29
Southern Illinois	28,674	2,658,210	92.70	1,100,574	38.38
Stanford	11,318	4,717,901	416.85	1,385,919	122.45
Syracuse	16,646	1,727,075	103.75	696,357	41.83
Tulane	8,811	1,223,167	138.82	475,441	53.96
Univ. Alabama	17,016	1,348,869	79.27	561,045	32.97

TABLE XXIX. (contd.)

University	Total Enrollment (FTE)	Total Library Expenditures	Per Capita Total Library Expenditures	Expenditures for Books, Per. Binding	Per Capita Expen. for Books, Per. Binding
Arizona	20,259[9]	1,441,952	71.18	552,960	27.29
California, Berkeley	27,819[10,18,27]	5,550,428	199.52	1,467,899	52.77
California, LA	29,070	5,319,670	183.00	1,534,932	52.80
Chicago	8,475	3,547,627	418.60	1,239,112	146.21
Colorado	17,107	2,040,689	119.29	792,922	46.35
Florida	16,393	1,802,231	109.94	580,349	35.40
Illinois[2]	28,651	4,077,979	142.33	1,699,351	59.31
Iowa	16,903	2,011,382	119.00	846,648	50.09
Kansas	15,833	1,670,976	105.54	678,677	42.86
Kentucky	13,547	1,652,960	122.02	670,878	49.52
Michigan	35,145	5,161,643	146.87	1,421,363	40.44
Minnesota	48,285	3,619,178	74.95	1,304,447	27.02
Missouri[3]	18,140[11]	1,802,000	99.34	810,000	44.65
Nebraska	20,215	1,362,166[47]	67.38	504,987[58]	24.98
North Carolina	15,591	2,091,040	134.12	824,065	52.86
Oklahoma	15,980	1,325,439	82.94	592,125	37.05
Pennsylvania	15,780	2,601,790	164.88	935,441	59.28
Rochester	5,606	1,921,125	342.69	546,978	97.57
Southern California	11,840	1,660,117	140.21	510,163	43.09
Texas	29,526[25]	3,013,128	102.05	698,785[59]	23.67
Toronto	28,369	6,720,501[49]	236.90	2,175,961	76.70
Virginia	8,570	1,551,167	181.00	600,983	70.13
Univ. Washington	38,462	3,194,301	83.05	870,359	22.63

TABLE XXIX. (contd.)

University	Total Enrollment (FTE)	Total Library Expenditures	Per Capita Total Library Expenditures	Expenditures for Books, Per. Binding	Per Capita Expen. for Books, Per. Binding
Wisconsin[4]	33,497	3,479,453	103.87	1,341,449	40.05
Washington Univ.	7,503	2,140,648	285.31	862,377	114.94
Wayne State	24,28,31 24,904	2,550,985	102.43	1,008,142	40.48
Yale	7,995	3,620,000	452.78	1,173,000	146.72
Total	994,740	141,258,935	--	47,685,800	--
No. of Libraries	50	50	50	50	50
Average	19,895	2,825,179	142.01	953,716	47.94

TABLE XXX. LIBRARY RESOURCES--VOLUMES AND CURRENT PERIODICALS
(TOTAL NUMBER AND PER STUDENT CAPITA)

University	Total Volumes (June 30, 1968)	Gross No. of Vols. Added (3-year Average)	Net No. of Vols. Added (3-year Average)	Current Periodicals Received	Volumes Per Student	Periodicals Per Student
Brown Univ.	1,239,899	44,299	42,886	7,850	252.58	1.60
Columbia	3,895,937	130,523	107,449	17,660	292.95	1.33
Cornell	3,257,399	191,475	176,410	25,557	225.11	1.77
Duke	1,944,554	79,470	75,900	9,961	298.34	1.53
Harvard	7,920,387	221,785	158,438	41,048	526.97	2.73
Indiana[1]	1,846,551	--	130,000	10,673	68.14	0.40
Johns Hopkins	1,767,383[62]	80,263	31,046	10,512[64]	242.01	1.44
Louisiana State[69]	1,045,454	45,747	44,550	16,199	54.48	0.84
M.I.T.	1,064,501	83,883	80,061	6,430	138.46	0.84
McGill	1,150,287	58,768	55,051	14,600	78.95	1.00
Michigan State	1,394,691	--	99,797	12,500	30.35	0.27
New York	1,534,610	83,020	75,215	12,000	68.84	0.54
Northwestern	1,936,782[62]	77,879	75,703	26,702	120.81	1.67
Ohio State	2,103,723	122,293	118,260	9,680	51.78	0.24
Pennsylvania State	1,164,142	113,448	108,597	9,528	32.66	0.27
Princeton	1,998,491	77,213	74,927	21,648[64]	423.50	4.59
Purdue	903,748	67,208	64,308	12,700	32.50	0.46
Rutgers	1,468,139	100,000	95,000	9,100	49.50	0.31
Southern Illinois	1,306,701	153,180	147,800	17,935	45.57	0.28
Stanford	3,070,812	192,500	164,161	40,232[64]	271.32	3.55
Syracuse	1,303,692	76,275	34,948	7,611	78.32	0.46
Tulane	984,258	37,268	11,182[68]	--	111.71	--
Univ. Alabama	942,893	--	65,930	7,937	55.41	0.47

TABLE XXX. (contd.)

University	Total Volumes (June 30, 1968)	Gross No. of Vols. Added (3-year Average)	Net No. of Vols. Added (3-year Average)	Current Periodicals Received	Volumes Per Student	Periodicals Per Student
Arizona	1,291,778	45,186	42,979	10,900	63.76	0.54
California, Berkeley	3,478,893	163,385	143,609	50,055[64]	125.05	1.80
California, LA	2,610,572	142,600	137,799	23,580	89.80	0.81
Chicago	2,712,785[63]	136,960	121,286	--	320.09	--
Colorado	1,202,337	--	85,211	13,000	70.28	0.76
Florida	1,273,515	64,303	62,441	9,972	77.69	0.61
Illinois[2]	4,086,854	204,233	195,739	19,052	142.64	0.66
Iowa	1,389,108	68,482	64,284	10,087	82.18	0.60
Kansas	1,344,739	75,918	74,197	11,887	84.93	0.75
Kentucky	969,360	69,001	67,844	10,000	71.56	0.74
Michigan	3,816,394	162,980	154,797	23,409[65]	108.59	0.67
Minnesota	2,691,202	123,553	113,198	14,852	55.74	0.31
Missouri[3]	1,400,000	75,000	72,000	--	77.18	--
Nebraska[70]	890,666	41,660	37,499	11,050[66]	44.06	0.55
North Carolina	1,821,756	78,783	75,652	5,649	116.85	0.36
Oklahoma	1,153,758	61,148	58,856	8,466	72.70	0.53
Pennsylvania	2,099,869	80,728	71,694	11,471	133.07	0.73
Rochester	1,139,753[63]	71,462	69,421	12,594	203.31	2.25
Southern California	1,290,862	54,826	50,683	8,830	109.03	0.75
Texas	2,036,000	112,166	111,005	8,706	68.96	0.29
Toronto[50]	2,907,274[63]	254,311	251,540	19,227[64]	102.48	0.68
Virginia	1,445,229	79,088[67]	74,625	7,696	168.64	0.90
Univ. Washington	1,641,130	103,517	100,762	17,049	42.67	0.44

TABLE XXX. (contd.)

University	Total Volumes (June 30, 1968)	Gross No. of Vols. Added (3-year Average)	Net No. of Vols. Added (3-year Average)	Current Periodicals Received	Volumes Per Student	Periodicals Per Student
Wisconsin[4]	2,012,329	124,878	--	16,280	60.07	0.49
Washington Univ.	1,078,655	69,673	65,961	10,200	143.76	1.36
Wayne State	1,110,592	77,349	70,321	9,028	44.59	0.36
Yale	5,318,971[63]	190,000	155,275	10,240	665.29	1.28
Total	99,459,415	4,767,687	4,566,297	692,543	--	--
No. of Libraries	50	46	49	47	50	47
Average	1,989,188	103,645	93,190	14,735	99.99	0.72

TABLE XXXI. LIBRARY RESOURCES--MICROFORMS

University	Total No. of Microforms	Microfilm Reels	Microfiche	Microcards	Microprint	Microfiche, Microcards, &Microprint
Brown Univ.	182,600	11,914	71,758	41,008	57,920	170,686
Columbia[71]	546,151	55,488	--	--	--	490,663
Cornell[71]	748,724	46,382	--	--	--	702,342
Duke[71]	139,667	22,000	--	--	--	117,667
Harvard	491,514	41,641	107,219	88,727	253,927	449,873
Indiana[1,71]	297,396	20,527	--	--	--	276,869
Johns Hopkins[72]	425,000	--	--	--	--	--
Louisiana State[69]	240,937	33,698	58,305	106,713	42,221	207,239
M.I.T.[71]	156,316	5,778	--	--	--	150,538
McGill[72]	157,890	--	--	--	--	--
Michigan State[73]	270,492	14,821	130,266	--	125,405	255,671
New York	502,230	13,262	226,380	168,288	94,300	488,968
Northwestern	259,213	13,737	35,250	107,895	102,331	245,476
Ohio State[71]	361,094	30,216	--	--	--	330,878
Pennsylvania State[73]	441,312	46,300	329,181	--	65,831	395,012
Princeton	308,204	35,785	19,268	50,356	202,795	272,419
Purdue	350,000	10,000	90,000	160,000	90,000	340,000
Rutgers[71]	118,820	17,620	--	--	--	101,200
Southern Illinois[71]	112,027	52,027	--	--	--	60,000
Stanford[71]	434,423	31,870	--	--	--	402,553
Syracuse[74]	924,704	17,173	111,179	796,352	--	907,531
Tulane	380,730	8,145	--	--	--	372,585
Univ. Alabama	262,972	10,540	--	--	--	252,432

TABLE XXXI. (contd.)

University	Total No. of Microforms	Microfilm Reels	Microfiche	Microcards	Microprint	Microfiche, Microcards, & Microprint
Arizona[71]	68,967	14,735	--	--	--	54,232[75]
California, Berkeley[71]	506,138	101,396	--	--	--	404,742
California, LA[71]	518,791	48,036	--	--	--	470,755
Chicago[63]	160,392	49,690	23,217	15,047	72,438	110,702
Colorado	17,284	4,645	1,337	10,357	945	12,639
Florida	86,504	45,514	5,350	24,460	11,180	40,990
Illinois[2,72]	317,601	--	--	--	--	--
Iowa	349,423	34,603	163,113	47,075	104,632	314,820
Kansas	64,886	16,891	726[76]	46,584	685[76]	47,995
Kentucky	606,598	41,623	181,607	210,559	172,809	564,975
Michigan[71]	450,523	55,759	--	--	--	394,764
Minnesota	359,893	49,048	95,680	94,651	120,514	310,845
Missouri[3,77]	--	--	--	--	--	--
Nebraska	7,641	2,452	33	4,426	730	5,189
North Carolina[71]	280,441	26,088	--	--	--	254,353
Oklahoma[72]	149,800	--	--	--	--	--
Pennsylvania	464,600	25,540	--	--	--	439,060
Rochester[78]	--	14,826	--[79]	--	--	--
Southern California	203,694	9,518	2,109	13,076	178,991	194,176
Texas	435,145[80]	27,930	71,490	69,130	266,595	407,215
Toronto[50,71]	356,720	23,860	--	--	--	332,860
Virginia	455,498	16,204	194,093	131,103	114,098	439,294
Univ. Washington[71]	603,375	32,367	--	--	--	571,008

TABLE XXXI. (contd.)

University	Total No. of Microforms	Microfilm Reels	Microfiche	Microcards	Microprint	Microfiche, Microcards, & Micropring
Wisconsin[4,71]	625,203	13,768	--	--	--	611,435
Washington Univ.[71]	335,044	14,126	--	--	--	320,918
Wayne State[71]	421,000	21,000	--	--	--	400,000
Yale[81]	--	--	--	--	--	--
Total	15,957,577	1,228,543	1,917,561	2,185,807	2,078,347	13,693,569
No. of Libraries	47	44	21	19	20	43
Average	339,523	27,921	91,312	115,042	103,917	318,455

TABLE XXXII. PERSONNEL--NUMBER AND DISTRIBUTION;
STUDENTS PER STAFF CAPITA

University	Total Staff Members (FTE)	Prof. Staff Members (FTE)	Percent Prof.	Clerical and Sub-Prof. (FTE)	Students Per Prof. Staff Member	Students Per Total Staff Member
Brown Univ.	154	54	35.1	100	90.91	31.88
Columbia	512	145	28.3	367[83]	91.72	25.97
Cornell	407	140	34.4	267	103.36	35.55
Duke	170	68	40.0	102	95.85	38.34
Harvard	653	227	34.8	426	66.21	23.02
Indiana[1]	219	97[82]	44.3	122[82]	279.36	123.74
Johns Hopkins	122	33	27.0	89	221.30	59.86
Louisiana State	109	51	46.8	58[84]	376.29	176.06
M.I.T.	200	65	32.5	135	118.28	38.44
McGill	297	92	40.0	205	158.36	49.05
Michigan State	167	68	40.7	99	675.72	275.14
New York	295	83	28.1	212	268.58	75.57
Northwestern	182	77	42.3	105	208.19	88.08
Ohio State	223	95	42.6	128	427.71	182.21
Pennsylvania State	359	99	27.6	260	360.09	99.30
Princeton	233	76	32.6	157	62.09	20.25
Purdue	173	64	37.0	109	434.44	160.72
Rutgers	138	64	46.4	74	463.42	214.92
Southern Illinois	154	79	51.3	75	362.96	186.19
Stanford	362	141	39.0	221	80.27	31.27
Syracuse	186	67	36.0	119	248.45	89.49
Tulane	98	39	39.8	59	225.92	89.91
Univ. Alabama	127	46	36.2	81	369.91	133.98

TABLE XXXII. (contd.)

University	Total Staff Members (FTE)	Prof. Staff Members (FTE)	Percent Prof.	Clerical and Sub-Prof. (FTE)	Students Per Prof. Staff Member	Students Per Total Staff Member
Arizona	103	45	43.7	58	450.20	196.69
California, Berkeley	399	168	42.1	231	165.59	69.72
California, LA	344	139	40.4	205	209.14	84.51
Chicago	270	86	31.9	184[85]	98.55	31.89
Colorado	172	53	30.8	119	322.77	99.46
Florida	185	73	39.5	112	224.56	88.61
Illinois[2]	347	163	47.0	184	175.77	82.57
Iowa	169	71	42.0	98	238.07	100.02
Kansas	163	61	37.4	102	259.56	97.13
Kentucky	137	56	40.9	81	241.91	98.88
Michigan	511	190	37.2	321	184.97	68.78
Minnesota	280	141	50.4	139	342.45	172.45
Missouri[3]	130	44	33.8	86	412.27	139.54
Nebraska	127	48	37.8	79	421.15	159.17
North Carolina	173	73	42.2	100	213.58	90.12
Oklahoma	112	37	33.0	75	431.89	142.68
Pennsylvania	263	91	34.6	172	173.41	60.00
Rochester	166	64	38.6	102	87.59	33.77
Southern California	161	64	39.8	97	185.00	73.54
Texas	223	94	42.2	129	314.11	132.40
Toronto	577	154	26.7	423	184.21	49.17
Virginia	148	47	31.8	101	182.34	57.91
Univ. Washington	305	106	34.8	199	362.85	126.10

TABLE XXXII. (contd.)

University	Total Staff Members (FTE)	Prof. Staff Members (FTE)	Percent Prof.	Clerical and Sub-Prof. (FTE)	Students Per Prof. Staff Member	Students Per Total Staff Member
Wisconsin[4]	266	88	33.1	178	380.65	125.93
Washington Univ.	184	56	30.4	128	133.98	40.78
Wayne State	178	65	36.5	113	383.22	139.91
Yale	487	192	39.4	295	41.64	16.42
Total	12,120	4,439	--	7,681	--	--
No. of Libraries	50	50	50	50	50	50
Average	242.4	88.8	36.6	153.6	224.09	82.07

TABLE XXXIII. PERSONNEL--NUMBER OF HOURS AND AMOUNT SPENT FOR HOURLY WAGES; STAFF WORK HOURS PER WEEK

University	Wages: No. of Hours	Wages: Amount	Work Hours Per Week Prof. Staff	Work Hours Per Week: Clerical & Subprof. Staff
Brown Univ.	74,200	108,157	37.5	37.5
Columbia	221,217	405,765	35.0	35.0
Cornell	198,283	350,561	39.0	39.0
Duke	69,935	92,394	39.5	40.0
Harvard	307,974	559,266	35.0	35.0
Indiana[1]	215,424	335,000	38.5	40.0
Johns Hopkins	60,000	45,700	37.5	37.5
Louisiana State	52,402	167,287	39.0	40.0
M.I.T.	37,106	62,950	35.0	37.5[87]
McGill	64,300	[53]	35.0	35.0
Michigan State	176,000	319,439[55]	40.0	40.0
New York	160,000	[52]	35.0	35.0
Northwestern	133,435	130,882	37.5	37.5
Ohio State	196,681	242,881	40.0	40.0
Pennsylvania State	200,758	298,587	40.0	40.0
Princeton	29,164	116,664	36.25	36.25
Purdue	--	79,143	40.0	40.0
Rutgers	154,260	[52]	38.5	35.0
Southern Illinois	251,608	310,852	37.5	40.0
Stanford	120,400	198,660	40.0	40.0
Syracuse	65,000	72,985	37.5	37.5
Tulane	80,190	78,545	40.0	40.0
Univ. Alabama	113,000	69,268[54]	39.0	39.0

TABLE XXXIII. (contd.)

University	Wages: No. of Hours	Wages: Amount	Work Hours Per Week: Prof. Staff	Work Hours Per Week: Clerical & Subprof. Staff
Arizona	118,229	137,492	39.0	39.0
California, Berkeley	284,782	683,283	40.0	40.0
California, LA	446,628	52	40.0	40.0
Chicago	162,608[85]	53	37.5	37.5
Colorado	116,000	129,882	40.0	40.0
Florida	92,827	121,393	40.0	40.0
Illinois[2]	183,340	203,269	39.0	40.0
Iowa	88,101	118,911	40.0	40.0
Kansas	104,924	117,987	40.0	40.0
Kentucky	78,420	83,029	40.0	40.0
Michigan	246,142	524,035	37.5	40.0
Minnesota	302,172	364,571	40.0	40.0
Missouri[3]	80,000	97,000	39.0	40.0
Nebraska	96,420	123,456	40.0	40.0
North Carolina	82,400	113,568	39.0	40.0
Oklahoma	68,107	276,372	40.0	40.0
Pennsylvania	96,878	157,980	35.0	35.0
Rochester	54,269	104,699	35.0	35.0
Southern California	78,298	127,344	40.0	40.0
Texas	196,900	244,641	40.0	40.0
Toronto[86]	31,868	53	36.25	36.25
Virginia	90,677	78,815	40.0	40.0
Univ. Washington	189,802	284,753	40.0	40.0

TABLE XXXIII. (contd.)

University	Wages: No. of Hours	Wages: Amount	Work Hours Per Week Prof. Staff	Work Hours Per Week: Clerical & Subprof. Staff
Wisconsin[4]	151,996	225,667	40.0	40.0
Washington Univ.	59,903	80,588	37.5	37.5
Wayne State	133,277	222,177	37.5	37.5
Yale	64,000	220,000	37.5	--
Total	6,680,305	8,885,898	1,922	1,894
No. of Libraries	49	44	50	49
Average	136,332	201,952	38.44	38.66

TABLE XXXIV. RELATIONSHIP OF NUMBER OF SEATS FOR READERS TO TOTAL ENROLLMENT

University	No. of Seats	Total Enrollment	Seating Capacity (Percent of Enrollment)	No. of Students Per Seat
Brown Univ.	1,432	4,909	0.29	3.43
Columbia	4,539	13,299	0.34	2.93
Cornell	4,872	14,470	0.34	2.97
Duke	3,448	6,518[12]	0.53	1.89
Harvard	6,979	15,030	0.46	2.15
Indiana[1]	7,808	27,098	0.29	3.47
Johns Hopkins	1,500	7,303[5,13]	0.21	4.87
Louisiana State	2,500	19,191	0.13	7.68
M.I.T.	1,737	7,688[29]	0.23	4.43
McGill	2,946	14,569	0.20	4.95
Michigan State	4,057	45,949	0.09	11.33
New York	3,000	22,292	0.13	7.43
Northwestern	2,014	16,031[7]	0.13	7.96
Ohio State	4,383	40,632	0.11	9.27
Pennsylvania State	2,968	35,649	0.08	12.01
Princeton	2,942	4,719	0.62	1.60
Purdue	3,337	27,804[14]	0.12	8.33
Rutgers	3,532	29,659[8,15,26]	0.12	8.40
Southern Illinois	3,000[91]	28,674	0.10	9.56
Stanford	4,251	11,318	0.38	2.66
Syracuse	1,100	16,646	0.07	15.13
Tulane	2,015	8,811	0.23	4.37
Univ. Alabama	2,325	17,016	0.14	7.32

TABLE XXXIV. (contd.)

University	No. of Seats	Total Enrollment	Seating Capacity (Percent of Enrollment)	No. of Students Per Seat
Arizona	1,471	20,259[9]	0.07	13.77
California, Berkeley	4,522	27,819[10,18,27]	0.16	6.15
California, LA	4,399	29,070	0.15	6.61
Chicago	2,409	8,475	0.28	3.52
Colorado[92]	1.783	17,107	0.10	9.59
Florida	2,650	16,393	0.16	6.19
Illinois[2]	3,952	28,651	0.14	7.25
Iowa	3,326	16,903	0.20	5.09
Kansas	2,334	15,833	0.15	6.78
Kentucky	3,257	13,547	0.24	4.16
Michigan[93]	6,698	35,145	0.19	5.25
Minnesota	7,039	48,285	0.15	6.86
Missouri[3]	3,000	18,140[11]	0.17	6.05
Nebraska	2,403	20,215	0.12	8.41
North Carolina	4,625	15,591	0.30	3.37
Oklahoma	2,925	15,980	0.18	5.46
Pennsylvania	4,500	15,780	0.29	3.51
Rochester	955	5,606	0.17	5.87
Southern California	2,587	11,840	0.22	4.58
Texas	4,695	29,526[25]	0.16	6.29
Toronto[94]	1,374	28,369	0.05	20.65
Virginia	1,813	8,570	0.21	4.73
Univ. Washington	4,413	38,462	0.11	8.72

TABLE XXXIV. (contd.)

University	No. of Seats	Total Enrollment	Seating Capacity (Percent of Enrollment)	No. of Students Per Seat
Wisconsin[4]	3,762	33,497	0.11	8.90
Washington Univ.	2,242	7,503	0.30	3.35
Wayne State	2,309	24,28,31 24,904	0.09	10.79
Yale	--	7,995	--	--
Total	162,074	986,745	--	--
No. of Libraries	49	49	49	49
Average	3,308	20,138	16	6.09

TABLE XXXV. SQUARE FEET AND LINEAR FEET OF
BOOK SHELVES; AND VOLUMES PER SQ. FT.

University	No. of Volumes	Linear Ft. of Shelves	Square Ft. for Shelves	Volumes per Sq. Ft.
Brown Univ.	1,239,899	314,148	151,684	8.17
Columbia	3,895,937	--	212,772	18.31
Cornell	3,257,399	--	237,715	13.70
Duke	1,944,554	--	135,283	14.37
Harvard	7,920,387	871,237	523,068	15.14
Indiana[1]	1,846,551	453,412	232,376	7.95
Johns Hopkins	1,767,383[62]	--	--	--
Louisiana State	1,045,454	121,440	--	--
M.I.T.	1,064,501	--	48,034	22.16
McGill	1,150,287	--	--	--
Michigan State	1,394,691	186,414	--	--
New York	1,534,610	--	--	--
Northwestern	1,936,782[62]	211,512[88]	117,147[90]	16.53
Ohio State	2,103,723	267,437	140,965	14.92
Pennsylvania State	1,164,142	176,500	--	--
Princeton	1,998,491	375,000	218,686	9.14
Purdue	903,748	159,884	89,595	10.09
Rutgers	1,468,139	--	--	--
Southern Illinois	1,306,701	131,541	74,785	17.47
Stanford	3,070,812	--	--	--
Syracuse	1,303,692	--	104,000	12.54
Tulane	984,258	229,446	121,162	8.12
Univ. Alabama	942,893	--	--	--

TABLE XXXV. (contd.)

University	Volumes	Linear Ft. of Shelves	Square Ft. for Shelves	Volumes per Sq. Ft.
Arizona	1,291,778	--	69,536	18.58
California, Berkeley	3,478,893	--	250,709	13.88
California, LA	2,610,572	--	231,622	11.27
Chicago	2,712,785[63]	--	--	--
Colorado[92]	1,202,337	16,580	24,070	49.95
Florida	1,273,515	210,536	94,317	13.50
Illinois[2]	4,086,854	--	239,168	17.09
Iowa	1,389,108	240,174	104,186	13.33
Kansas	1,344,739	--	139,027	9.67
Kentucky	969,360	340,400	121,582	7.97
Michigan[93]	3,816,394	548,425	268,460	14.22
Minnesota	2,691,202	725,358	362,679	7.42
Missouri[3]	1,400,000	--	--	--
Nebraska	890,666	171,714[89]	90,042	9.89
North Carolina	1,821,756	--	81,374	22.39
Oklahoma	1,153,758	--	81,311	14.19
Pennsylvania	2,099,869	--	--	--
Rochester	1,139,753[63]	67,446	38,824	29.36
Southern California	1,290,862	238,219	143,612	8.99
Texas	2,036,000	462,026	209,266	9.73
Toronto[94]	2,907,274[63]	--	77,648	37.44
Virginia	1,445,229	368,387	150,248	9.62
Univ. Washington	1,641,130	273,521	109,408	15.00

TABLE XXV. (contd.)

University	Volumes	Linear Ft. of Shelves	Square Ft. for Shelves	Volumes per Sq. Ft.
Wisconsin[4]	2,012,329	--	152,101	13.23
Washington Univ.	1,078,655	180,763	83,181	12.97
Wayne State	1,110,592	200,000	80,000	13.88
Yale	5,318,971[63]	--	--	--
Total	99,459,415	7,541,520	5,609,643	--
No. of Libraries	50	26	37	37
Average	1,989,188	290,058	151,612	13.26

TABLE XXXVI. AMOUNT OF STAFF AREA AND
SQUARE FEET PER STAFF MEMBER

University	Sq. Ft. of Staff Area	Total No. of Staff Members	Sq. Ft. per Staff Member
Brown Univ.	28,158	154	182.84
Columbia	11,632	512[83]	22.72
Cornell	49,224	407	120.94
Duke	30,000	170	176.47
Harvard	91,287	653	139.80
Indiana[1]	50,304	219[82]	229.70
Johns Hopkins	--	122	--
Louisiana State	--	109[84]	--
M.I.T.	20,540	200	102.70
McGill	--	297	--
Michigan State	--	167	--
New York	--	295	--
Northwestern	--	182	--
Ohio State	36,213	223	162.39
Pennsylvania State	34,500	359	96.10
Princeton	35,780	233	153.56
Purdue	30,173	173	174.41
Rutgers	--	138	--
Southern Illinois	20,632	154	133.00
Stanford	--	362	--
Syracuse	9,000	186	48.39
Tulane	26,135	98	266.68
Univ. Alabama	--	127	--

TABLE XXXVI. (contd.)

University	Sq. Ft. of Staff Area	Total No. of Staff Members	Sq. Ft. per Staff Member
Arizona	--	103	--
California, Berkeley	--	399	--
California, LA	--	344	--
Chicago	--	270[85]	--
Colorado	13,194	172	76.71
Florida	10,405	185	56.24
Illinois[2]	29,858	347	86.05
Iowa	35,104	169	207.72
Kansas	28,797	163	176.67
Kentucky	32,455	137	236.90
Michigan	82,769	511	161.97
Minnesota	79,397	280	283.56
Missouri[3]	15,000	130	115.38
Nebraska	20,714	127	163.10
North Carolina	20,000	173	115.61
Oklahoma	--	112	--
Pennsylvania	--	263	--
Rochester	8,800	166	53.01
Southern California	27,242	161	169.20
Texas	45,648	223	204.70
Toronto	66,123	577	114.60
Virginia	48,657	148	328.76
Univ. Washington	24,875	305	81.56

TABLE XXXVI. (contd.)

University	Sq. Ft. of Staff Area	Total No. of Staff Members	Sq. Ft. per Staff Member
Wisconsin[4]	42,734	266	160.65
Washington Univ.	21,948	184	119.28
Wayne State	17,500	178	98.31
Yale	--	487	--
Total	1,144,798	8,343	--
No. of Libraries	34	34	34
Average	33,671	245.38	137.22

TABLE XXXVII. TOTAL AND PER CAPITA GENERAL AND RESERVE CIRCULATION

University	General Circulation	General Circulation (Per Capita)	Reserve Circulation	General and Reserve Circulation	General and Reserve Circulation (Per Capita)
Brown Univ.	284,658	57.99	122,857	407,515	83.01
Columbia	847,104[95]	63.70	561,611[103]	1,408,715	105.93
Cornell	773,568	53.46	476,327	1,249,895	86.38
Duke	318,028[96]	48.79	161,281[96]	479,309	73.54
Harvard	--	--	--	1,020,262	67.88
Indiana[1]	--	--	--	1,350,000	49.82
Johns Hopkins	170,000	23.28	40,000	210,000	28.76
Louisiana State	181,097	9.44	15,369	196,466	10.24
M.I.T.	229,966	29.91	41,897	271,863	35.36
McGill	--	--	--	801,041	54.98
Michigan State	484,319	10.54	357,158	841,477	18.31
New York	362,902	16.28	448,100	811,002	36.38
Northwestern	162,143	10.11	100,366	262,509	16.38
Ohio State	--	--	--	1,388,691	34.18
Pennsylvania State	663,042	18.60	97,737	760,779	21.34
Princeton	391,573	82.98	123,661	515,234	109.18
Purdue	380,674	13.69	244,606	625,280	22.49
Rutgers	127,723[97]	4.31	--[104]	--	--
Southern Illinois	810,562	28.27	189,108[105]	999,670	34.86
Stanford	691,691	61.11	342,623	1,034,314	91.39
Syracuse	--	--	--	--	--
Tulane	490,997	55.73	34,157	525,154	59.60
Univ. Alabama	599,018	35.20	--	--	--

TABLE XXXVII. (contd.)

University	General Circulation	General Circulation (Per Capita)	Reserve Circulation	General and Reserve Circulation	General and Reserve Circulation (Per Capita)
Arizona	357,726	17.66	270,823[106]	628,549	31.03
California, Berkeley	--	--	--	2,361,329	84.88
California, LA	1,790,755	61.60	198,905[107]	1,989,660	68.44
Chicago	507,086	59.83	391,389	898,475	106.01
Colorado	624,935	36.53	152,866	777,801	45.47
Florida	922,214	56.26	37,628[108]	959,842	58.55
Illinois[2]	914,880	31.93	647,860	1,562,740	54.54
Iowa	235,328	13.92	171,857	407,185	24.09
Kansas	409,256	25.85	123,087	532,343	33.62
Kentucky	156,578	11.56	37,875	194,453	14.35
Michigan	994,866[98]	28.31	268,568[109]	1,263,434	35.95
Minnesota	697,013	14.44	366,004	1,063,017	22.02
Missouri[3]	--	--	--	--	--
Nebraska	154,721[99]	7.65	38,322[99]	193,043	9.55
North Carolina	495,003	31.75	88,238	583,241	37.41
Oklahoma	556,646	34.83	53,980	610,626	38.21
Pennsylvania	446,706	28.31	--[110]	--	--
Rochester	432,592	77.17	122,408	555,000	99.00
Southern California	317,010	26.77	174,696	491,706	41.53
Texas	2,395,029	81.12	122,675[111]	2,517,704	85.27
Toronto	971,928	34.26	426,519	1,398,447	49.29
Virginia	201,382	23.50	59,714	261,096	30.47
Univ. Washington	972,536[100]	25.29	543,175	1,515,711	39.41

TABLE XXXVII. (contd.)

University	General Circulation	General Circulation (Per Capita)	Reserve Circulation	General and Reserve Circulation	General and Reserve Circulation (Per Capita)
Wisconsin[4]	464,153[101]	13.86	321,840	785,993	23.46
Washington Univ.	277,119[102]	36.93	235,713[102]	512,832	68.35
Wayne State	325,742	13.08	211,220	536,962	21.56
Yale	560,280	70.08	39,970	600,250	75.08
Total	24,150,549	--	8,462,190	38,360,615	--
No. of Libraries	43	43	40	45	45
Average	561,641	28.93	211,555	852,458	42.74

TABLE XXXVIII. PUBLIC SERVICE DATA--MISCELLANEOUS

University	No. of Hours Open Per Week*	Attendance Statistics
Brown Univ.	103	728,348
Columbia	80.5[113]	--
Cornell	107	720,552[123]
Duke	94-106	--
Harvard	75-93	--
Indiana[1]	109	--
Johns Hopkins	112	745,511
Louisiana State	103.5	--
M.I.T.	102[114]	--
McGill	80.5	1,530,279
Michigan State	103	--
New York	88	--
Northwestern	87[115]	--
Ohio State	106.25	1,359,781[124]
Pennsylvania State	106.5	1,075,326
Princeton	106	--
Purdue	111	2,288,829
Rutgers	106.5	--
Southern Illinois	108	--
Stanford	94	--
Syracuse	92	--
Tulane	91.25	--
Univ. Alabama	100.75	--

TABLE XXXVIII. (contd.)

University	No. of Hours Open Per Week	Attendance Statistics
Arizona	106	--
California, Berkeley	87-102	--
California, LA	101.25	1,932,928[107]
Chicago	84-91.5	--
Colorado	119[116]	1,238,500[125]
Florida	99-105	--
Illinois[2]	87[117]	1,334,418[126]
Iowa	121.5	970,427
Kansas	78[118]	--
Kentucky	108	--
Michigan	101[119]	2,854,120[109]
Minnesota	93	--
Missouri[3]	102	--
Nebraska	78[120]	--
North Carolina	92.5	--
Oklahoma	103	--
Pennsylvania	96	--
Rochester	88	--
Southern California	74[121]	--
Texas	79-107	--
Toronto[112]	95.5	811,085[127]
Virginia	98	--
Univ. Washington	89.5	--

TABLE XXXVIII. (contd.)

University	No. of Hours Open Per Week	Attendance Statistics
Wisconsin[4]	122 88-120	--
Washington Univ.	100	--
Wayne State	87	128 1,976,000
Yale	96	--
Total	4,877.25	19,566,104
No. of Libraries	50	14
Average	97.55	1,397,578

*Where a range of hours is indicated, the mid-point is used in determining the average.

LAW LIBRARIES

TABLES XXXIX - XLV

TABLE XXXIX. SUMMARY DATA ON LAW LIBRARIES

	No. of Libs.	Total Amount	Average	Range Low	First Quartile	Median	Third Quartile	Range High
Enrollment (FTE)	30	17,248	574.93	296	363	501	607	1,707
Faculty (FTE)	30	944.88	31.50	13.0	21.0	27.15	40.0	72.0
Volumes	30	6,158,704	205,290	53,273	97,676	162,570	202,300	1,132,935
Volumes per Student	30		357.07	130	180	325	410	843
Current Journals	30	54,196	1,806.53	300	520	996.00	2,000	7,500
Journals per Student	30		3.14	0.6	1.3	2.5	3.8	10.5
Professional Staff	30	188.45	6.28	1.75	3.5	5.25	8.0	21.1
Non-professional Staff	30	268.10	8.94	1.00	3.00	5.75	13.00	38.9
Total Staff	30	456.55	15.22	4.00	7.00	11.25	20.00	56.5
Students per Staff Member	30		37.78	15	30	46	75	111
Expenditures for Books	30	2,179,245	72,642	27,000	42,225	72,099	91,896	183,009
Book Expen. per Student	30		126.35	42.49	96.42	118.86	171.74	314.49
Salary Expenditures	30	3,139,581	104,653	25,198	41,763	68,139	156,111	393,386
Salary Expen. per Student	30		182.03	69.16	90.67	137.34	252.47	419.89
Hours of Opening per Week	29	2,852.25	98.35	67.00	89.75	98.00	104.75	168.00

TABLE XL. LAW LIBRARIES: ENROLLMENT, FACULTY, VOLUMES AND JOURNALS (INSTITUTIONAL RANK)

University	Enrollment (FTE)	Faculty (FTE)	Volumes	Volumes per Student	Current Periodicals	Current Periodicals per Student
Columbia	3	3.5	2	6	13	21
Duke	25	18.5	16	7	18	13
Harvard	1	1	1	2	4	13
Indiana	16	16	20	20	10	8
McGill	26.5	30	30	26	11	6
Rutgers	11	3.5	10	15	9	9.5
Stanford	18	12	14	10	5	2
Syracuse	24	29	28	27	28	24.5
Tulane	22	27	17	13	19	15
Univ. Alabama	30	18.5	25	18	24	19
Arizona	28	24	26	22	29	24.5
California, LA	9	7	12	17	6	5
Chicago	17	21	6	3	3	1
Florida	7	10	23	28	22	27
Illinois	8	15	9	16	12	13
Iowa	20	18.5	15	8	15	11
Kansas	29	27	22	12	27	23
Kentucky	14	27	24	24	25	28
Michigan	4	6	4	9	1	4
Minnesota	10	14	5	4	8	9.5
North Carolina	15	8.5	18	21	30	30
Oklahoma	23	24	27	25	23	21
Pennsylvania	12	13	7	11	14	17.5

TABLE XL. (contd.)

	Enrollment (FTE)	Faculty (FTE)	Volumes	Volumes per Student	Current Periodicals	Current Periodicals per Student
Southern California	26.5	22	21	14	21	17.5
Texas	2	5	8	29	2	7
Toronto	19	18.5	29	30	17	16
Virginia	5	8.5	11	19	16	21
Univ. Washington	21	24	13	5	7	3
Wisconsin	6	11	19	23	20	26
Yale	13	2	3	1	26	29
Total	17,248	944.88	6,158,704	--	54,196	--
No. of Libraries	30	30	30	30	30	30
First Quartile	363	21.0	97,676	180	520	1.3
Median	501	27.15	162,570	325	996	2.5
Third Quartile	607	40.0	202,300	410	2,000	3.8

TABLE XLI. LAW LIBRARIES: STAFF
(INSTITUTIONAL RANK)

University	Prof. Staff	Non-Prof. Staff	Total Staff	Students Per Staff Member
Columbia	16.5	6.5	8.5	11
Duke	9.5	29.5	18	17
Harvard	2	1	1	23
Indiana	25.5	27	27	2
McGill	14.5	9.5	12	27.5
Rutgers	12	15	15	12.5
Stanford	12	5	7	26
Syracuse	30	22	29	6
Tulane	25.5	16.5	18	15.5
Univ. Alabama	16.5	22	18	20
Arizona	23	18	20	18
California, LA	9.5	9.5	10	22
Chicago	7.5	2	3	30
Florida	20	22	22	3
Illinois	12	14	14	14
Iowa	14.5	16.5	16	19
Kansas	25.5	29.5	29	8
Kentucky	20	22	22	9
Michigan	1	4	2	24
Minnesota	5.5	12	11	21
North Carolina	25.5	25	25	4
Oklahoma	28	27	29	5
Pennsylvania	7.5	6.5	6	25

TABLE XLI. (contd.)

University	Prof. Staff	Non-Prof. Staff	Total Staff	Students Per Staff Member
Southern California	20	22	22	15.5
Texas	3	13	8.5	10
Toronto	29	19	26	7
Virginia	20	11	13	12.5
Univ. Washington	4	8	5	29
Wisconsin	20	27	24	1
Yale	5.5	3	4	19
Total	188.45	268.10	456.55	--
No. of Libraries	30	30	30	30
First Quartile	3.5	3.00	7.00	30
Median	5.25	5.75	11.25	46
Third Quartile	8.0	13.00	20.00	75

TABLE XLII. LAW LIBRARIES: EXPENDITURES AND LIBRARY
HOURS (INSTITUTIONAL RANK)

University	Expenditures for Books	Book Expen. per Student	Salary Expenditure	Salary Expen. per Student	Hours of Opening Per Week
Columbia	4	20	4	7	22
Duke	14	4	18	14	8
Harvard	3	26	1	10	23.5
Indiana	18	18	27	30	13
McGill	30	25	14	8	28
Rutgers	1	2	12	12	16
Stanford	2	1	10	4	7
Syracuse	28	19	30	29	18
Tulane	21	16	23	19	14.5
Univ. Alabama	26	14	22	15	20.5
Arizona	12	3	24	17	10
California, LA	8	11	6	6	5.5
Chicago	6	5	5	3	14.5
Florida	22	27	20	28	9
Illinois	5	9	17	20	18
Iowa	11	6	15	13	18
Kansas	23	13	26	18	25
Kentucky	19	24	21	24	5.5
Michigan	24	30	2	7	11
Minnesota	10	12	9	9	1
North Carolina	17	17	19	21	29
Oklahoma	29	23	28	27	27
Pennsylvania	9	10	8	5	23.5

-97-

TABLE XLII. (contd.)

University	Expenditures for Books	Book Expen. for Student	Salary Expenditure	Salary Expen. per Student	Hours of Opening Per Week
Southern California	27	25	29	26	26
Texas	15	29	11	23	20.5
Toronto	25	21	25	25	1
Virginia	16	22	13	16	3
Univ. Washington	13	7	7	2	12
Wisconsin	20	28	16	22	2
Yale	7	8	3	1	4
Total	2,179,245	--	3,139,581	--	2,852.25
No. of Libraries	30	30	30	30	30
First Quartile	42,225	96.42	41,763	90.67	89.75
Median	72,099	118.86	68,139	137.34	98.00
Third Quartile	91,896	171.74	156,111	252.47	104.75

TABLE XLIII. LAW LIBRARIES: ENROLLMENT, FACULTY, VOLUMES
AND JOURNALS (INSTITUTIONAL DATA)

University	Enrollment (FTE)	Faculty (FTE)	Volumes	Volumes per Student	Current Journals	Current Journals per Student
Columbia	1,000	45	480,000	480	1,381	1.4
Duke	339	25	157,278	464	813	2.4
Harvard	1,707	72	1,132,935	664	4,047	2.4
Indiana	490	27	119,755	244	1,877	3.8
McGill	325	13	53,273	164	1,681	5.2
Rutgers	583	45	190,000	326	1,900	3.3
Stanford	442	35	168,274	381	4,010	9.1
Syracuse	343	13.5	55,614	162	386	1.1
Tulane	371	16	131,895	356	770	2.1
Univ. Alabama	296	25	89,874	304	463	1.6
Arizona	305	21	72,000	236	325	1.1
California, LA	604	41	186,537	309	3,818	6.3
Chicago	448	24	252,918	565	4,724	10.5
Florida	656	37.25	97,676	149	570	0.9
Illinois	607	27.3	196,806	324	1,473	2.4
Iowa	395	25	161,762	410	1,000	2.5
Kansas	298	16	107,000	359	395	1.3
Kentucky	519	16	92,773	179	424	0.8
Michigan	979	44	380,010	388	7,500	7.7
Minnesota	600	31	309,487	516	2,000	3.3
North Carolina	512	40	121,977	238	300	0.6
Oklahoma	363	21	63,815	176	520	1.4
Pennsylvania	563	33	204,648	363	1,058	1.9

TABLE XLIII. (contd.)

	Enrollment (FTE)	Faculty (FTE)	Volumes	Volumes per Student	Current Journals	Current Journals per Student
Southern California	325	23	108,777	335	607	1.9
Texas	1,414	44.83	202,300	143	5,800	4.1
Toronto	422	25	54,923	130	845	2.0
Virginia	730	40	189,263	259	992	1.4
Univ. Washington	385	21	185,989	483	3,440	8.9
Wisconsin	668	36	120,145	180	677	1.0
Yale	559	62	471,000	843	400	0.7
Total	17,248	944.88	6,158,704	--	54,196	--
No. of Libraries	30	30	30	30	30	30
Average	574.93	31.50	205,290	357.07	1,806.53	3.14

TABLE XLIV. LAW LIBRARIES: EXPENDITURES AND
LIBRARY HOURS (INSTITUTIONAL DATA)

University	Expenditures for Books	Book Expenditure Per Student	Salary Expenditures	Salary Expenditure Per Student	Hours of Opening Per Week
Columbia	110,856	101.86	192,460	192.46	90.5
Duke	76,822	226.61	55,092	162.51	104.5
Harvard	125,000	73.23	393,386	230.45	89
Indiana	57,141	116.61	33,889	69.16	99.5
McGill	27,000	83.08	82,054	252.47	78
Rutgers	183,009	313.91	112,000	192.11	95
Stanford	139,004	314.49	139,747	316.17	105
Syracuse	36,000	104.96	25,198	73.46	94
Tulane	43,903	118.34	41,763	112.57	98
Univ. Alabama	39,903	134.81	45,563	153.93	92
Arizona	78,500	257.38	36,400	119.34	103
California, LA	91,896	152.15	164,584	272.49	108
Chicago	100,971	225.38	180,349	402.56	98
Florida	43,813	66.79	48,265	73.57	104.2
Illinois	102,067	168.15	63,800	105.11	94
Iowa	80,791	204.53	70,634	178.82	94
Kansas	42,225	141.69	35,016	117.50	85
Kentucky	44,998	86.70	46,690	89.96	108
Michigan	41,600	42.49	258,700	264.25	102
Minnesota	87,431	145.72	143,563	239.27	168
North Carolina	60,000	117.19	52.563	102.66	67
Oklahoma	35,000	96.42	27,176	74.87	81
Pennsylvania	88,995	158.07	156,111	277.28	89

TABLE XLIV. (contd.)

University	Expenditures for Books	Book Expenditure Per Student	Salary Expenditures	Salary Expenditure Per Student	Hours of Opening Per Week
Southern California	38,800	119.38	25,208	77.56	82
Texas	73,000	51.63	128,205	90.67	92
Toronto	41,439	98.20	35,360	83.79	--
Virginia	71,197	97.53	88,148	120.75	110
Univ. Washington	77,884	202.30	157,294	408.56	101
Wisconsin	44,000	65.87	65,643	98.27	112
Yale	96,000	171.74	234,720	419.89	108.5
Total	2,179,245	--	3,139,581	--	2,852.25
No. of Libraries	30	30	30	30	29
Average	72,642	126.35	104,653	182.03	98.35

TABLE XLV. LAW LIBRARIES: STAFF
(INSTITUTIONAL DATA)

University	Prof. Staff	Non-Prof. Staff	Total Staff	Students per Staff Member
Columbia	5	15	20.00	50
Duke	7	1	8.00	42
Harvard	17.6	38.9	56.50	30
Indiana	3	2	5.00	98
McGill	5.5	12	17.50	19
Rutgers	6	6	12.00	49
Stanford	6	16.5	22.50	20
Syracuse	1	3	4.00	86
Tulane	3	5	8.00	46
Univ. Alabama	5	3	8.00	37
Arizona	3.5	4	7.50	41
California, LA	7	12	19.00	32
Chicago	8	22.2	30.20	15
Florida	4	3	7.00	94
Illinois	6	7	13.00	47
Iowa	5.5	5	10.50	38
Kansas	3	1	4.00	75
Kentucky	4	3	7.00	74
Michigan	21.1	18.5	39.60	25
Minnesota	9	9	18.00	33
North Carolina	3.0	2.5	5.50	93
Oklahoma	2	2	4.00	91
Pennsylvania	8	15	23.00	24
Southern California	4	3	7.00	46

TABLE XLV. (contd.)

University	Prof. Staff	Non-Prof. Staff	Total Staff	Students per Staff Member
Texas	12	8	20.00	71
Toronto	1.75	3.5	5.25	80
Virginia	4	11	15.00	49
Univ. Washington	10.5	13	23.50	16
Wisconsin	4	2	6.00	111
Yale	9	21	30.00	19
Total	188.45	268.10	456.55	--
No. of Libraries	30	30	30	30
Average	6.28	8.94	15.22	37.78

MEDICAL LIBRARIES

TABLES XLVI - LII

TABLE XLVI. SUMMARY DATA ON MEDICAL LIBRARIES

	No. of Libs.	Total Amount	Average	Range Low	First Quartile	Median	Third Quartile	Range High
Enrollment (FTE)	25	21,607	864.28	32	468	628.00	1,055	2,712
Faculty (FTE)	24	11,880	495.00	30	209	342	525	2,379
Volumes	25	3,505,042	140,202	15,378	106,623	77,267	176,870	437,550
Volumes per Student	25		162.22	18.2	86.6	160.6	316.7	880.1
Current Journals	25	52,692	2,107.68	226	1,414	1,825	2,550	6,275
Journals per Student	25		2.44	0.3	1.2	2.5	5.35	61
Professional Staff	25	182.75	7.31	1.00	4.5	6	8.5	29.5
Non-professional Staff	25	328.80	13.15	1.00	7.5	11.	15.6	58.2
Total Staff	25	511.55	20.46	3.50	13.5	17.0	22.5	87.7
Students per Staff Member	25		42.24	2.0	21.6	41.5	82.7	241.7
Expenditures for Books	25	1,572,427	62,897	12,525	39,868	57,377	83,372	195,551
Book Expenditure per Student	25		72.77	5.42	38.57	86.36	135.28	2,812.50
Salary Expenditure	25	3,244,308	129,772	15,000	82,923	101,802	141,336	550,289
Salary Expenditure per Student	25		150.15	17.73	83.08	161.29	320.26	3,212.50
Hours of Opening/Week	24	2,325.25	96.89	81.50	89.25	95	104	118.00

TABLE XLVII. MEDICAL LIBRARIES: ENROLLMENT, FACULTY,
VOLUMES, AND JOURNALS (INSTITUTIONAL RANK)

University	Enrollment (FTE)	Faculty (FTE)	Volumes	Volumes per Student	Current Periodicals	Current Periodicals Per Student
Columbia	4	2	3	11.5	6	17
Duke	21	23	17	8	13	6
Harvard	12	7	1	3	2	3
McGill	9	20	9	14	8	13.5
Northwestern	16	--	7	7	9	9
Ohio State	13	1	18	16	15	13.5
Stanford	18	21	5	4	7	8
Tulane	17	18	15	11.5	14	10
Arizona	25	24	24	1	10	1
California, LA	8	12	4	9	1	4
Florida	6	19	11	19	18	19
Illinois	2	4	6	20	12	22.5
Iowa	5	15	19	21	21	20.5
Kentucky	11	17	14	17	11	16
Michigan	1	10	8	23	5	20.5
North Carolina	3	8	12	22	22	24
Oklahoma	20	16	21	13	24	22.5
Pennsylvania	14	3	23	24	19	15
Rochester	23	6	16	6	16	7
Southern California	24	9	22	10	23	11
Toronto	10	5	25	25	25	25
Virginia	19	13	20	15	20	12

TABLE XLVII. (contd.)

University	Enroll-ment (FTE)	Faculty (FTE)	Volumes	Volumes per Student	Current Periodicals	Current Periodicals Per Student
Univ. Washington	22	22	10	5	3	2
Wisconsin	7	14	13	18	17	18
Yale	15	11	2	2	4	5
Total	21,607	11,880	3,505,042	--	52,692	--
No. of Libraries	25	24	25	25	25	25
First Quartile	468	209	77,267	86.6	1,414	1.2
Median	628	342	106,623	160.6	1,825	2.5
Third Quartile	1,055	525	176,870	316.7	2,550	5.35

TABLE XLVIII. MEDICAL LIBRARIES: STAFF
(INSTITUTIONAL RANK)

University	Prof. Staff	Non-Prof. Staff	Total Staff	Students per Staff Member
Columbia	7	4	4	10
Duke	5.5	12.5	9	20
Harvard	1	1	1	24
McGill	15	8	9	11
Northwestern	10.5	20	18.5	14
Ohio State	24	21	23	6
Stanford	22	7	11	19
Tulane	5.5	25	21	8
Arizona	15	15.5	15	25
California, LA	2.5	3	3	18
Florida	15	18	18.5	7
Illinois	10.5	12.5	12	3
Iowa	21	23	24	2
Kentucky	10.5	15.5	13	9
Michigan	18.5	5	6	4
North Carolina	15	14	14	5
Oklahoma	10.5	18	16.5	17
Pennsylvania	23	11	16.5	13
Rochester	15	6	7	23
Southern California	20	22	22	16
Toronto	25	24	25	1
Virginia	18.5	18	20	15

TABLE XLVIII. (contd.)

University	Prof. Staff	Non-Prof. Staff	Total Staff	Students per Staff Member
Univ. Washington	8	10	9	21
Wisconsin	4	9	5	12
Yale	2.5	2	2	22
Total	182.75	328.80	511.55	--
No. of Libraries	25	25	25	25
First Quartile	4.5	7.5	13.5	21.6
Median	6.0	11.0	17.0	41.5
Third Quartile	8.5	15.6	22.5	82.7

TABLE XLIX. MEDICAL LIBRARIES: EXPENDITURES AND LIBRARY HOURS (INSTITUTIONAL RANK)

University	Expenditures for Books	Book Expenditure Per Student	Salary Expenditures	Salary Expenditure Per Student	Hours of Opening Per Week
Columbia	8	17	5	17	17
Duke	3	2	9	6	5.5
Harvard	1	5	1	2	13
McGill	20	19	10	16	18
Northwestern	21	16	19	14	19
Ohio State	22	21	22	19	22
Stanford	16	11	11	8	14
Tulane	17	12	18	12	16
Arizona	6	1	12	1	1
California, LA	2	9	2	7	8
Florida	15	18	21	20	15
Illinois	5	20	6	21	24
Iowa	24	24	24	23	12
Kentucky	12	14	14	18	3
Michigan	23	25	13	24	11
North Carolina	13	22	15	22	20
Oklahoma	14	7	16	9	22
Pennsylvania	10	10	17	15	4
Rochester	18	6	7	3	5.5
Southern California	7	4	23	10	7
Toronto	25	23	25	25	--
Virginia	19	13	20	13	10

TABLE XLIX. (contd.)

University	Expenditures for Books	Book Expenditure Per Student	Salary Expenditures	Salary Expenditure Per Student	Hours of Opening Per Week
Univ. Washington	4	3	8	5	22
Wisconsin	11	15	4	11	9
Yale	9	8	3	4	2
Total A	1,572,427	--	3,244,308	--	2,325.25
No. of Libraries	25	25	25	25	24
First Quartile	39,868	38.57	82,923	83.08	89.25
Median	57,377	86.36	101,802	161.29	95.0
Third Quartile	83,372	135.28	141,336	320.26	104.0

TABLE L. MEDICAL LIBRARIES: ENROLLMENT, FACULTY
VOLUMES, AND JOURNALS (INSTITUTIONAL DATA)

University	Enroll-ment (FTE)	Faculty (FTE)	Volumes	Volumes per Student	Current Journals	Current Journals per Student
Columbia[129]	1,370	2,043	285,000	208.0	2,736	2.0
Duke	332	40.3	89,679	270.1	1,825	5.5
Harvard	772	450	437,550	566.8	5,308	6.9
McGill	886	187	130,389	147.2	2,177	2.5
Northwestern	552	--	171,156	310.1	2,150	3.9
Ohio State[130]	628	2,379	82,920	132.0	1,600	2.5
Stanford	499	84	222,452	445.8	2,363	4.7
Tulane	504	244	104,833	208.0	1,641	3.3
Arizona[131]	32	30	28,164	880.1	1,952	61.0
California, LA[132]	974	350	225,453	231.5	6,275	6.4
Florida[134]	1,136	209	116,118	102.2	1,512	1.3
Illinois	2,551	691	182,584	71.6	1,882	0.7
Iowa	1,216	298	81,730	67.2	1,335	1.1
Kentucky[135]	840	248	104,876	124.9	1,904	2.3
Michigan	2,712	404	166,154	61.3	3,000	1.1
North Carolina	1,703	441	109,030	64.0	1,055	0.6
Oklahoma	439	250	70,501	160.6	300	0.7
Pennsylvania[136]	623	886	33,386	53.6	1,469	2.4
Rochester	305	525	98,000	321.3	1,597	5.2
Southern California	273	423	60,995	223.4	860	3.2
Toronto[137,138]	846	614	15,378	18.2	226	0.3
Virginia	496	333	72,804	146.8	1,358	2.7

TABLE L. (contd.)

University	Enrollment (FTE)	Faculty (FTE)	Volumes	Volumes per Student	Current Journals	Current Journals per Student
Univ. Washington[139]	326	80	120,731	370.3	3,393	10.4
Wisconsin	1,014	316	106,623	105.2	1,551	1.5
Yale	578	355	388,536	672.2	3,223	5.6
Total	21,607	11,880	3,505,042	--	52,692	--
No. of Libraries	25	24	25	25	25	25
Average	864.28	495	140,202	162.22	2,107.68	2.44

TABLE LI. MEDICAL LIBRARIES: STAFF
(INSTITUTIONAL DATA)

University	Prof. Staff	Non-Prof. Staff	Total Staff	Students per Staff Member
Columbia[129]	8	21	29.0	47.2
Duke	9	11	20.0	16.6
Harvard	29.5	58.2	87.7	8.8
McGill	6	14	20.0	44.3
Northwestern	7	7	14.0	39.4
Ohio State[130]	2	5.5	7.5	83.7
Stanford	3.5	15.1	18.6	26.8
Tulane	9	1	10.0	50.4
Arizona[131]	6	10	16.0	2.0
California, LA[132]	12	23	35.0	27.8
Florida[134]	6	8	14.0	81.1
Illinois	7.0	11.0	18.0	141.7
Iowa	3.75	3	6.75	180.1
Kentucky[135]	7	10	17.0	49.4
Michigan	5	18	23.0	117.9
North Carolina	6.0	10.5	16.5	103.2
Oklahoma	7	8	15.0	29.3
Pennsylvania[136]	3	12	15.0	41.5
Rochester	6	16	22.0	13.9
Southern California	4	5	9.0	30.3
Toronto[137,138]	1	2.5	3.5	241.7
Virginia	5	8	13.0	38.2
Univ. Washington[139]	7.5	12.5	20.0	16.3

TABLE LI. (contd.)

University	Prof. Staff	Non-Prof. Staff	Total Staff	Students per Staff Member
Wisconsin	10.5	13.5	24.0	42.3
Yale	12	25	37.0	15.6
Total	182.75	328.80	511.55	--
No. of Libraries	25	25	25	25
Average	7.31	13.15	20.46	42.24

TABLE LII. MEDICAL LIBRARIES: EXPENDITURES
AND LIBRARY HOURS (INSTITUTIONAL DATA)

University	Expenditures for Books	Book Expenditure per Student	Salary Expenditures	Salary Expenditure Per Student	Hours of Opening Per Week
Columbia[129]	73,265	53.48	167,780	122.47	90.5
Duke	97,557	293.85	118,692	357.51	105
Harvard	195,551	253.30	550,289	712.81	95
McGill	36,903	41.65	110,360	124.56	90
Northwestern	32,490	58.86	85,846	155.52	89.5
Ohio State[130]	21,688	34.54	65,899	104.93	87
Stanford	49,609	99.42	109,020	218.48	94.5
Tulane	44,872	89.03	86,849	172.32	92
Arizona[131]	90,000	2,812.50	102,800	3,212.50	118
California, LA[132]	113,684	116.72	275,640	283.00	101.25
Florida[134]	54,400	47.89	69,558	61.23	93
Illinois	90,500	35.48	145,198	56.92	81.5
Iowa	12,680	10.43	49,320	40.56	97
Kentucky[135]	61,977	73.78	101,473	120.80	108
Michigan	14,689	5.42	101,807	37.54	98
North Carolina	57,377	33.70	94,525	55.50	89
Oklahoma	56,382	128.43	89,349	203.53	87
Pennsylvania[136]	68,369	109.74	88,833	142.59	106
Rochester	43,335	142.08	137,534	450.93	105
Southern California	76,743	281.11	51,995	190.46	103
Toronto[137,138]	12,525	14.80	15,000	17.73	--
Virginia	42,833	86.36	80,000	161.29	99

TABLE LII. (contd.)

University	Expenditures for Books	Book Expenditure per Student	Salary Expenditures	Salary Expenditure Per Student	Hours of Openings Per Week
Univ. Washington[139]	93,766	287.63	123,447	378.67	87
Wisconsin	62,232	61.37	188,374	185.77	100.5
Yale	69,000	119.38	234,720	406.09	108.5
Total	1,572,427	--	3,244,308	--	2,325.25
No. of Libraries	25	25	25	25	24
Average	62,897	72.77	129,772	150.15	96.89

MISCELLANEOUS TABLE
LIII

TABLE LIII. STAFF ELIGIBILITY, BENEFITS, AND STATUS

University	Vacations and Holidays[140] Professional Staff	Vacations and Holidays[140] Clerical Staff	Status of Professional Staff	Professional Staff Eligibility Sabbaticals	Study Leaves	Retirement Benefits	Hospital Insurance	Meeting Time and Travel	Permanent Tenure	Criteria for Appointment
Brown Univ.	24 W.D.	24 W.D.	Academic	Some	Some	Yes	Yes	Yes	Yes	M.S.L.S.
Columbia	23 W.D. 12 H.	10-20[141] 12 H.	Academic	No	Some	Yes	Yes	Some	No	M.S.L.S.[142]
Cornell	22 W.D. 8 H.	15 W.D. 8 H.	Academic	No	Some	Yes	Yes	Some	No	M.L.S.[143]
Duke	20 W.D. 5 H.	10-20[141] 5 H.	Faculty, Admin. & Academic	Some	Yes	Yes	Yes	Yes	No	Lib.Degree[144]
Harvard	32	25	Admin.	No	Some	Yes	Yes	Some	Yes	Lib.Degree[145]
Indiana, Bloomington	22 W.D. 7 H.	10-15[141] 7 H.	Faculty & Academic	Some		Yes	Yes	Yes	Yes	5th year Lib.Degree[146]
Johns Hopkins	22 W.D.	22 W.D.	"Not stated"	No	Some	Yes	Yes	Yes	Some	Lib.Degree[147]
Louisiana State	9-11 H. 22 W.D. 14 H.	12-18 W.D.[141] 14 H.	Faculty[148]	Yes	Yes	Yes	Yes	Yes	Yes	L.S.Degree
M.I.T.	20	10-20 W.D.[141]	Admin.	No	Some	Yes	Yes	Some	No	M.S.L.S.[149]
McGill	22 W.D.	15 W.D.	Nonacademic	No	Some	Yes	Yes	Some	No	Lib.Degree[150]
Michigan State	21	11	Academic	Yes	Yes	Yes	Yes	Yes	No	Lib.Degree[151]
New York	22 W.D. 15 H.	10-20[141] 15 H.	Admin. & Faculty	Some	Some	Yes	Yes	Yes	Yes	M.L.S.
Northwestern	23 W.D.[152]	15 W.D.[152]	Admin.	Some	Some	Yes	Yes	Some	No[153]	M.L.S.
Ohio State	30	19	Faculty & Special[154]	No	Yes	Yes	Yes	Some	Yes	M.L.S.

-119-

TABLE LIII. (contd.)

-120-

University	Vacations and Holidays[140] Professional Staff	Vacations and Holidays[140] Clerical Staff	Status of Professional Staff	Professional Staff Eligibility Sabbaticals	Study Leaves	Retirement Benefits	Hospital Insurance	Meeting Time and Travel	Permanent Tenure	Criteria for Appointment
Penn. State	33	21	Academic	Yes	Yes	Yes	Yes	Yes	Yes	M.L.S.
Princeton	22 W.D. 10.5 H.	22 W.D. 10.5 H.	Academic	Yes	Yes	Yes	Yes	Yes	No	
Purdue	22	10	Faculty	Yes	Yes	Yes	Yes	Yes	Yes	[156]
Rutgers	23 W.D. 6 H.	15-20 W.D.[141] 10 H.	Faculty	No	Yes	Yes	Yes	Some	Some	Master's Degree[157]
Southern Illinois	20 W.D. 6 H.	10-20 W.D.[141] 6 H.	Faculty	Yes	Yes	Yes	Yes	Yes	Yes	[158]
Stanford	20	15-20[141]	Academic	Some	Yes	Yes	Yes	Yes	No	M.L.S.
Syracuse	22	10	Academic[159]	No	Some	Yes	Yes	Some	No	M.S.L.S.[160]
Tulane	22 W.D. 9 H.	15 W.D. 9 H.	Faculty	No	Yes	Yes	Yes	Yes	Yes	Competence[161]
Univ. Alabama	46	30	Academic	Yes	No	Yes	Yes	Some	Yes	M.L.S.
Arizona	30	30	Faculty	Yes	Some	Yes	Yes	Yes	Yes	M.L.S.[162]
California, Berkeley	24	15-24[141]	Academic[163]	No	Some	Yes	Yes	Some	No	M.L.S.
California, LA	24	15-24[141]	Academic	No	No	Yes	Yes	Some	No	M.L.S.
Chicago	20 W.D. 7 H.	15 W.D. 7 H.	Academic	No	Yes	Yes	Yes	Yes	Yes	Lib.Degree[164]
Colorado	22	10-20[141]	Faculty	Yes	Yes	Yes	Yes	Some	Yes	M.L.S.[165]
Florida	22 W.D. 8 H.	20-26[141]	Faculty	No	Yes	Yes	Yes	Yes	Yes	5th Year Lib.Degree

TABLE LIII. (contd.)

University	Vacations and Holidays[140] Professional Staff	Clerical Staff	Status of Professional Staff	Professional Staff Eligibility							
				Sabbaticals	Study Leaves	Retirement Benefits	Hospital Insurance	Meeting Time and Travel	Permanent Tenure	Criteria for Appointment
Illinois, Urbana Champaign	23 W.D. 6 H.	12-25[141]	Faculty	Yes	No	Yes	Yes	Yes	Yes	M.L.S.
Iowa	29	12-27[141]	Academic	No	Yes	Yes	Yes	Some	Some	Lib.Degree
Kansas	24	12-28[141]		Yes	Yes	Yes	Yes	Yes	Yes	M.L.S.
Kentucky	22 W.D. 10 H.	10-15[141] 10 H.	Faculty	Yes	?	Yes	Yes	Yes	Yes	M.L.S.[166]
Michigan	24	12-24[141]	Academic	No	Yes	Yes	Yes	Some	No	M.L.S.[167]
Minnesota	22 W.D. 9 H.	12-15[141] 9 H.	Faculty & Civil Service[168]	Some[169]	Some[169]	Yes	Yes	Yes	Yes	M.L.S.
Missouri, Columbia	8	8	Nonacademic	Some	Some	Yes	Yes	Yes	Yes	M.L.S.
Nebraska	24 W.D. 6 H.	10-15[141] 6 H.	Faculty	No	Yes	Yes	Yes	Yes	Yes	M.L.S.
North Carolina	31	24	Academic	No	Some	Yes	Yes	Some	Some	M.L.S.
Oklahoma	22 W.D. 6 H.	10 W.D. 6 H.	Faculty	Yes	Some	Yes	Yes	Some	Yes	M.L.S.
Pennsylvania	22 W.D. 8 H.	18-28[141] 8 H.	Admin.	No	Yes	Yes	Yes	Yes	No	Lib.Degree[170]
Rochester	20 W.D. 9 H.	10-15[141] 9 H.	Academic	No	Yes	Yes	Yes	Yes	Yes	M.L.S.
Southern California	30	20	Faculty[171]	Yes	Yes	Yes	Yes	Yes	Yes	M.L.S.
Texas at Austin	22-25[141]	22-25[141]	Nonacademic[172]	Yes	No	Yes	Yes	Yes	No	M.L.S.

-121-

TABLE LIII. (contd.)

University	Vacations and Holidays[140] Professional Staff	Clerical Staff	Status of Professional Staff	Professional Staff Eligibility							Criteria for Appointment
				Sabbaticals	Study Leaves	Retirement Benefits	Hospital Insurance	Meeting Time and Travel	Permanent Tenure	
Toronto	21 W.D.	10-20 W.D.[141]	Admin.	Yes	Yes	Yes	Yes	Yes	Some	Lib.Degree[174]
Virginia	12-18[141] 11 H.	12-18[141] 11 H.	Faculty or[173] Civil Service	No	Yes	Yes	Yes	Yes	No	M.L.S.[174]
Univ. Washington	34	22	Academic		Yes	Yes	Yes	Yes	No	
Wisconsin, Madison	22 W.D. 7.5 H.	10	Faculty, Academic, Civil Service	No	Some	Yes	Yes	Yes	Some	M.L.S.
Washington Univ.	22 W.D. 9 H.	10-22[141] 9 H.	Academic	No	Yes	Yes	Yes	Yes	No	M.L.S.[175]
Wayne State	30	20-30	Academic	Yes	Yes	Yes	Yes	Yes	Yes	M.L.S.
Yale	35	35	Admin.	Some	Some	Yes	Yes	Yes	No	176

-122-

FOOTNOTES

1. Data for Indiana University are for the Bloomington campus only.
2. Data for the University of Illinois are for the Urbana-Champaign campus only.
3. Data for the University of Missouri are for the Columbia campus only.
4. Data for the University of Wisconsin are for the Madison campus only.
5. Includes 1,894 day students and 2,289 FTE evening students (undergraduates).
6. Total number of students; not given for separate categories.
7. Part-time students are calculated as 0.50 FTE each.
8. Includes 6,616 part-time students calculated as 0.50 FTE each (undergraduates).
9. First semester, 1967-68; 15 units considered full load.
10. Fall quarter, 1967.
11. Total full-time students, Fall 1967. Source: School and Society, Jan. 6, 1968.
12. For degree students, those received in June, 1968.
13. Includes 134 day students and 731 FTE evening students (Master's candidates).
14. For 1966/67.
15. Includes 1,984 part-time students calculated as 0.50 FTE each (Master's candidates
16. Includes master's, professional degree, doctoral candidates, and "other" students.
17. Combined figure for Master's and Doctor's.
18. All graduates less Advanced Doctoral students are reported as Master's candidates.
19. Total graduate (Master's and Doctoral candidates) and including business are reported as master's candidates.
20. Included in figure for Doctoral candidates (Graduate College enrollment).
21. Total Graduate enrollment (Master's and Doctoral candidates, and professional).
22. Total Graduate enrollment (Master's and Doctoral candidates).
23. Total graduate enrollment (Master's and Doctoral candidates).
24. Includes 4,187 part-time calculated at 0.50 each (Master's candidates).
25. Law only included in Professional Degree candiates; precise number of degree candidates for other professional schools not available.

FOOTNOTES (contd.)

26. Includes full-time, part-time, and professional degree candidates (Doctoral candidates).

27. Advanced Doctoral students only are reported as Doctoral candidates.

28. Includes 274 part-time calculated at 0.50 each (Doctoral candidates).

29. Post-doctoral are not considered students but as post-doctoral associates and are included as "others" in the academic staff (total number in 1966/67: 224).

30. "Other" students are included in undergraduate and graduate categories.

31. Includes 710 part-time calculated at 0.50 each (Other students).

32. Includes 500 adjunct and clinical members counted as 250 FTE.

33. Assistant and above; does not include emeritus or N.Y. City Medical and Nursing.

34. 2,509 Full-time plus 3,171 part-time calculated as 0.50 FTE each.

35. Fall 1967; full-time, not FTE.

36. Includes 1,072 part-time calculated at 0.50 each.

37. Includes 3,060 part-time faculty calculated at 0.50 each.

38. University expenditures: Homewood Division, Arts and Sciences.

39. Includes College of Medicine; excludes University of Omaha.

40. Central Library only.

41. Includes building operation and maintenance, and contributions to pensions, etc.

42. Excludes expenditures for Argonne National Laboratory.

43. Main campus only.

44. Excludes all federal, grant, and gift funds.

45. For 1966-67; A.R.L. data.

46. Library expenditure includes $692,167 for building operation and maintenance, and $474,028 in contributions to pensions, etc.

47. Excludes University of Omaha; includes College of Medicine.

48. Main campus only.

49. Includes central and branch libraries.

FOOTNOTES (contd.)

50. Central and other libraries combined.
51. 1966-67 data.
52. Salary and wage expenditure combined.
53. No separate figures available.
54. Excludes work-study students.
55. Includes $50,677 for work-study.
56. Salaries only.
57. Combined expenditures for books, periodicals, and binding.
58. Includes commercial binding account only.
59. Pamphlet and temporary binding not included.
60. Excludes Business Administration Library.
61. Does not include fringe.
62. A.R.L. Academic Library Statistics, 1967-68.
63. Microforms included in volume count.
64. Periodicals and serials; not counted separately.
65. Excludes duplicates.
66. Includes duplicates.
67. Average of two years.
68. Reflects both withdrawals and a reduction due to a recount.
69. Main Library and Chemistry branch.
70. Includes College of Medicine, Omaha.
71. No separate breakdown by microfiche, microcards, and microprint available.
72. Total microform count only; no breakdown by categories.
73. Microfiche and microcard categories combined.
74. Microcard and microprint categories combined.
75. Excludes NASA and AEC holdings.
76. Boxes.

FOOTNOTES (contd.)

77. No figures on microforms available.
78. A count of volumes in microtext form is kept and added to total volume count.
79. Government documents on microfiche are not counted.
80. 8,746,295 "original manuscripts (documents)" not included.
81. Separate figures for microforms not kept, but are included in total volume count.
82. Budgeted positions, 1968-69.
83. Includes FTE of number of hours of student assistance and other hourly employees.
84. Includes 9.0 FTE Library Trainees.
85. Non-student hourly employees are included as clerical and subprofessional staff.
86. Central Library only.
87. Range = 35 - 40.
88. Estimated as no. of vols./10; or for Med. Lib., no. of vols./5.
89. Based, in part, as no. of vols./6.
90. Chicago and Evanston campuses; bookstack areas only.
91. Upon occupancy of present construction.
92. For Norlin Library only.
93. Includes new spaces under construction and new spaces for which funding is assured.
94. Central Library only.
95. Includes all loans for four or more days, all ILL, and all manuscripts loaned for photoduplication purposes (including in-house duplication).
96. Not including Law and Medical Libraries.
97. Central Library only.
98. Home use only.
99. Love Library only.
100. Includes both general and reserve Law Library circulation.

FOOTNOTES (contd.)

101. In general library.

102. Excludes Law Library.

103. Defined as circulation made for three days or less, excluding manuscripts loaned for photoduplication purposes.

104. No records of reserve circulation kept.

105. Two hour reserves; at Carbondale only.

106. Includes building use transactions.

107. For University Research Library and college libraries only.

108. July through April.

109. General library and undergraduate library only.

110. No reserve circulation figure; largely open reserve.

111. Closed reserves in main reading room only.

112. Main Library only.

113. Central circulation, etc.; other small units open longer.

114. Student Center Library open 24 hours/day.

115. 4,524 hours/52 weeks.

116. 17 hours/day times 7 days.

117. General Library Hours; departmental libraries varied from 35 to 107 hrs./week.

118. 4,101 hours/52 weeks.

119. Undergraduate Library 121 hrs./week.

120. 4,100 hrs./52 weeks.

121. 54 hrs./week for recesses and intersession; undergraduate library, in the general library remains open an additional 15 hrs./week when classes are in session.

122. 88 for service; 120 for study.

123. Olin Library only.

124. Main building only.

125. Norlin building use.

126. Turnstile in four departmental libraries only (Commerce, Physical Education, Undergraduate, Education).

FOOTNOTES (contd.)

127. Includes central stack entrance count of 565,587 and central reading room counts made six times daily.

128. 37,000 - 38,000 per sample week in General Library times 52 weeks.

129. Figures are for core Medical Library only; they do not include such units as the Institute of Cancer Research Library.

130. Figures are for "Health Center."

131. Figures reflect first year of operation of new medical school.

132. Biomedical Library.

133. Figures are for main medical library only; older medical publications are housed in Biology Library.

134. Health Center Library figures.

135. Includes medical, dental, pharmacy, nursing and allied health services.

136. Faculty includes 841 part-time calculated at 0.50 each.

137. Enrollment excludes undergraduate students; includes anatomy, biochemistry, pathology, psychiatry; excludes pharmacy and nursing.

138. Faculty includes 726 part-time calculated at 0.50 each.

139. Figures for the Library include dentistry.

140. Vacation and academic holiday allowances (total number of days); W.D.-work days; H.-holidays.

141. Number of days depends upon length of service.

142. Occasionally degree is waived in view of language or subject specialties.

143. Or specialized subject field.

144. Also, for some positions, higher degrees in subject fields.

145. In some positions specialized subject training or special experience is an acceptable substitute.

146. Or equivalent experience, and foreign language background.

147. Or equivalent experience.

148. Equivalent faculty rank.

149. Or equivalent education and experience.

150. Or specialization.

151. Or other higher degree for special appointments.

FOOTNOTES (contd.)

152. Holidays as approved by the University President.
153. "Continuing appointment" status after a period of three years.
154. "The University Libraries may recommend appointment to the faculty ranks and . . . special ranks."
155. May be waived in exceptional cases.
156. "Appropriate education; appropriate experience."
157. Ordinarily MLS degree.
158. Same as for teaching faculty, with some exceptions for the doctorate requirement.
159. Director has faculty status; others, academic.
160. Or, in some cases, master's degree in subject area.
161. As judged by Library Director or department head.
162. Or fifth-year professional degree for specialists.
163. Status is in process of being precisely defined on a University-wide level.
164. Or equivalent subject experience or training.
165. In some areas, a subject master's in addition to the M.L.S.
166. May be waived in exceptional cases.
167. Or equivalent in subject field.
168. Beginning librarians are appointed under Civil Service rules. Higher level or specialist's appointments are under academic regulations with faculty status.
169. Academic staff only; *supra.*, n. 29.
170. Or advanced subject degree.
171. Faculty privileges and rights but not rank.
172. Librarian, Associate Librarian, and Assistant Librarian are voting members of faculty.
173. Faculty rank at the level of department head and above.
174. Or state certification examination.
175. Or subject master's; special subject or bibliographic competence.
176. College and library school degrees.

Z
675
45D63

APR 26 1971